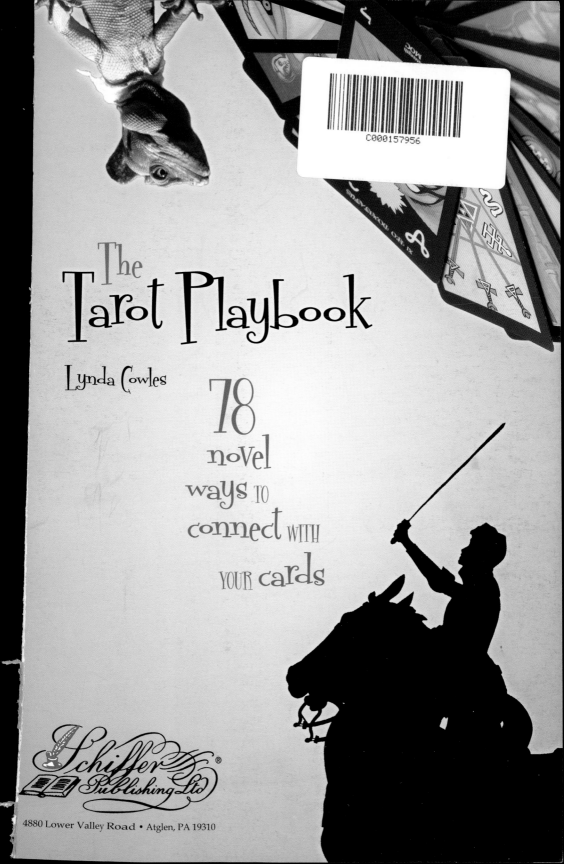

The Tarot Playbook

Lynda Cowles

78 novel ways to connect with your cards

Schiffer Publishing Ltd

4880 Lower Valley Road • Atglen, PA 19310

Designed by John P. Cheek
Cover design by Bruce Waters

Type set in Fontdinerdotcom/Book Antiqua

ISBN: 978-0-7643-3988-2
Printed in China

For my husband Tim:
My Magician, Emperor, Chariot, and Sun.

Acknowledgments

I would like to thank: Dinah Roseberry and Schiffer Publishing, for "getting" this book and helping me to get it out there; Janet Boyer, for convincing me to stop talking and start writing; Marilotte Adriani, for reading that early writing and saying nice things about it; Alison Kaefer, for being a one-woman cheering squad and all-round good gal; and Elspeth Christie, for her unflinching support of all my harebrained schemes over the last few years.

A big thank you to my parents for their love and encouragement, and to my brother Rob for instructing me in the art of writing utter nonsense. If it wasn't for him, this book would be so much duller.

Finally and totally, thank you to Tim for being my best friend, and Rachel for showing me there's more to life than Tarot (yes, really).

Contents

Introduction

Why Your Deck Wants You to Read This Book

It's the age old story: Tarot reader meets deck, they fall in love – bluebirds sing, hotdogs dance in formation. But, after a time, for one reason or another, things don't work out and they're forced to go their separate ways. The Tarot reader heads for the nearest metaphysical store, and the deck resigns itself to a life of neglect and anonymity.

BUT IT DOESN'T HAVE TO BE THIS WAY.

Your deck spent months, possibly years, in creation. Your deck wants to shine – to be handled, appreciated, and used as much as possible. It has so much it wants to share with you, if only you'd give it the opportunity. Your deck knows it deserves to be celebrated, not pushed to the back of a drawer. Deep down, you know it, too. *The Tarot Playbook* is designed to bring you and your deck closer together. From that awkward first meeting to happily ever after, this book will help you and your deck become Best Friends Forever.

Let's be honest. The time and effort required to study a new deck – to learn its ins and outs, to understand where it's coming from and where it's going – is often too tall an order to reach. Yet without this understanding, a Tarot deck can never be more than a stand–in, a cardboard cut–out substitute for some other deck. (You know, the one that you're *really* picturing in your head when you do a reading.)

Fortunately, *The Tarot Playbook* is here to help. No more must you commit to months of intensive study just to get to know a deck; no longer must you feel guilty for those decks buried in your underwear drawer. With *The Tarot Playbook*, every deck can have its day. I'm not talking about some 78-week-long homework assignment or a boot-camp-style schedule of daily draws and journal entries. That's work, and work is No Fun. Now you've bought *The Tarot Playbook*, every minute spent with your deck will be playtime!

In these pages, you will find 78 fun things that you and your deck can do together. Start at the beginning and proceed in an orderly fashion or pick and choose as the mood takes you. Whichever method you choose, you'll find plenty to keep you and your deck occupied without ever having to struggle through a reading or spend hours researching the alchemical emblems of early-Twentieth-century Masonic-cat-worshippers. And before you know it, you and your deck will have bonded, and will be able to read each other's minds and make each other coffee just how you like it.

Honest.

Sharing Your Life With Your Deck

You can't help but get closer to your deck by trying the activities in this book. But if you're really serious about this relationship and you want it to last forever – like those beautiful, romantic love affairs you see in the movies every day – you must commit yourself fully, with mind, body, and soul.

What happens when you finish a reading? Chances are you put your deck back in its box/bag/luxury custom-built cradle and go off to do something else. Think for a moment how that makes your deck feel. Would you like it if your friends only hung out with you when they wanted something from you? Even if you're a professional reader who spends hours every day with your deck, you should still make the effort to spend quality time with it outside office hours. Make sure it knows you love it for who it is – not just what it can do for you.

Take it with you everywhere you go. But don't just keep it in your bag or pocket – let it see the sights! Lay it on the passenger seat while you're driving, or buy a special basket for it to sit in when you're riding your bike. Talk to it about where you're going and what you can see. Keep it by your side at work and when you go out with your three-dimensional friends for drinks or a bite to eat. Give it a spot on the sofa when you're watching TV or – better yet – hold it in your hands so you can give it a loving shuffle every now and then. And when bedtime comes, don't forget to kiss your deck good night. Tuck it under your pillow, safe and sound, and when you wake up in the morning, draw one card to ask it how it slept.

If all this sounds like madness, you're starting to get a feel for the contents of this book, wherein you'll find plenty of irreverent, silly, and downright ridiculous things to do with your cards. But, in all seriousness, time spent with your deck is never wasted. The most amazing readings can occur when Tarot reader and deck are totally in sync, and isn't that, after all, what it's all about?

How to Use This Book

The Tarot Playbook has been cleverly structured so you can use it exactly as you choose. You can work – sorry, I mean *play* – through the activities one-by-one from beginning to end or you can dip in at random whenever you feel like hanging with your deck. You can choose to concentrate on a particular chapter – focusing on just the court cards, for example – or you can flick to one of the playlists at the back of the book, such as "Things to Do With Non–Scenic Pips," "Things to Do in a Hurry," and "Things to Do With Friends."

You can also let your deck choose what you do. Each activity is designated for one of the 78 Tarot cards so all you have to do is shuffle your deck, draw a card and refer to the Card Index at the back of the book.

As you approach each activity, you may be tempted to skip all the non-essential bits – you know, the parts that advise you to stand on your head whilst shuffling or to sew your Tarot cards into your clothes. However, you must do your very best to resist this temptation. Silliness is close to godliness, as they say, and the idea behind all these missions implausible is for you to step outside your comfort zone to see your cards in a different light. How can you ever get to know the King of Swords properly if you've never danced under the moonlight with him in your underwear? (Pop quiz: Did you just picture the King of Swords *wearing* your underwear or *tucked into* your underwear?)

Besides, when all is said and done, being silly is fun, and fun is…well, FUN! Just ask the Fool…

Keeping a Journal

As you spend time with your deck, you might like to keep a record of the activities you do, to preserve your thoughts and insights about the cards and to help you get to know them better.

Well, don't. Nothing sucks the fun out quicker than paperwork. Resist the temptation to buy a beautiful, hand–stitched hardback journal filled with creamy white pages. I know you want it, but you really don't need it. After all, would you take notes when you were spending time with your human friends? Do you think you would feel any closer to them if you did? (Well, maybe you would, but only in a creepy stalker kind of way.)

That said, many activities will go more smoothly if you have something with which to write. For this, I recommend an old reporter's note pad and a cheap Biro. That way, you won't be tempted to start again if your handwriting goes a bit squiffy. And when you've finished playing, you can just tear out the page and throw it away. In fact, you must.

If you spend enough time with your deck, you can't help but get to know it. Talk to it, play with it, take it for a walk in the park. But don't, whatever you do, try to analyze it. You'll only scare it away.

Playing With Difficult Decks

There are hundreds, nay, thousands of Tarot decks out there and every deck is different. Because of that, it's extremely unlikely that all of the activities in this book will suit your particular deck. Perhaps your deck doesn't have scenic minors, or perhaps one activity is all about clothing and your Tarot deck only features naked mermen. If so, feel free to customize any activity as much as you need. They are, after all, merely suggestions.

On the other hand, you could have one of those serious decks which refuses point blank to join in with anything it deems silly or immature. If this is your deck, don't worry. Not every activity in this book is silly. As it happens, those that appear to be complete nonsense are, in fact, cleverly disguised study aids specifically designed to help you appreciate the incredible intelligence, wisdom, and – dare I say – handsomeness of your unique and masterful deck. However, if your deck doesn't fall for *that*, just flick to the special playlist at the back of the book, entitled: "Sensible Things to Do With Serious Decks."

One More Thing...

For convenience (and my sanity) I refer to the Minor Arcana suits as Wands, Cups, Swords, and Pentacles throughout this book. I also call the Major Arcana cards by their traditional names (whatever that means). I apologize if you've got one of those new–fangled (or old–fangled, or feminist–fangled, or vampire–fangled) decks that uses different naming conventions.

Now, don't just sit there. Go and play!

First Contact

24 Ways to Get Acquainted With Your Cards

Committed

The Fool

Making a commitment to spend 78 days, weeks, or any length of time with a deck you've only just met is surely one of the most foolish things you can do. What if you don't get on? What if, after just one study session together, you realize you've made a terrible, terrible mistake? Your only choice is to suffer or fail. That's why this book exists. The only thing that is required of you and your cards is an open heart and a willingness to act like a fool...

1. This ceremony can be performed at any time of year, though Springtime is best.
2. Before you begin, some preparations must be made. Dress in whatever makes you feel most attractive. Wrap your cards in a white silk cloth or large white handkerchief. Light a candle.
3. Place your cards on a high surface, such as a table or a kitchen worktop. Lightly rest your left hand on top of your cards.
4. Now, say these words:

> I do solemnly declare, that I know of no good reason why I (say your name), should not frolic with wild abandon with you (say your deck's name), from this day forward for as long as either of us cares to – forsaking no others, and with no strings attached, for no other purpose than to enjoy each other's company and have a good time.

5. Unwrap your deck and allow it time to say the same to you (telepathically, of course).
6. Now cradle the cards in your hands and blow out the candle. The ceremony is complete. You and your deck have taken the first step towards present happiness. Celebrate by asking a random passer-by to take a photograph of the two of you together.

Twenty Questions

The Magician

What's this? A test? No fair! Ah, but life – and Tarot – is never fair. You may be yearning to start the bonding process with your deck but, before you do, this quiz will challenge any preconceptions that may be lurking in your subconscious. What you don't know might surprise you, and what you *do* know might surprise you even more...

1. Put your deck away. Do not look through the cards, do not put them anywhere you can see them, do not sneakily peek out of the corner of your eye. You may think no one is watching, but the Tarot gods see all.
2. Set a timer for five minutes.
3. Answer the 20 questions at right, making a note of your answers. When your time is up, immediately stop writing and put down your pencil.
4. Now check your answers against your cards. Don't beat yourself up if you got most of them wrong, for it was Socrates who said, "The only true wisdom is in knowing you know nothing." If this describes you, congratulations! You are a wise fool indeed.

Questions:

- What are the names of each of the suits in the Minor Arcana?
- Are the scales of Justice balanced or unbalanced?
- How many people are shown in the 10 of Pentacles?
- Does Death carry a scythe?
- How are the court cards ranked? (i.e., Page or Princess? Son or Valet?)
- Is the Empress pregnant?
- Are there any people shown in the 8 of Wands – if so, how many?
- In the Major Arcana, is Strength or Justice numbered VIII?
- Which way does the Ace of Swords point? Up or down?
- Does the Fool have a dog?
- How many cups are upright in the 5 of Cups?
- Is the High Priestess holding a book? If so, is it open or closed?
- Is the King of Swords sitting or standing?
- How many people are shown in the Lovers card?
- Are there any bandages shown in the 9 of Wands?
- What animal – if any – is depicted in Strength?
- Is the Knight of Wands riding a horse?
- How many stars are in the sky in the Star card?
- Does any liquid flow from the Ace of Cups?
- What, if anything, is pictured in the four corners of the World card?

First Impressions

The High Priestess

Before you fall head over heels in love with your deck, take a step back to examine its flaws. Be honest: There are cards you love and cards that, well, you don't. It's okay to have these feelings. There are things about you that your deck finds repulsive too but, in time, these very same things may be what you love most about each other. Maybe…

1. Look through the deck and select your absolute favorite and least favorite cards for each of the categories below.
2. Take a few moments to think about your choices. Why did you select each card as your favorite or least favorite? What about it do you particularly love or hate?
3. Make a note of your choices on a piece of paper then fold it three times and place it inside the box your cards came in. Return to it in a month's time. Have your feelings changed?

What is Your Favorite/Least Favorite:

- Major Arcana card?
- Minor Arcana suit?
- Ace?
- Numbered Wands card?
- Numbered Cups card?
- Numbered Swords card?
- Numbered Pentacles card?
- Numbered Minor Arcana card overall?
- Wands court card?
- Cups court card?
- Swords court card?
- Pentacles court card?
- Page?
- Knight?
- Queen?
- King?
- Court card overall?
- Card in the whole deck bar none?

Sweet Nothings

The Empress

It is a truth universally acknowledged that flattery will get you everywhere. Just as your partner loves compliments and your boss puffs at praise, so too will your deck appreciate being appreciated. Writing a letter to your deck, telling it how you feel and sharing with it your hopes and dreams, will help to create an intimate bond of trust and mutual respect. Which can only be a good thing, right?

1. Nobody wants a love letter that's been written on the back of an envelope, so choose a nice sheet of paper (perhaps in a color that complements your deck) and dig out your best pen. You might like to spread the deck out in front of you for inspiration as you write.
2. Tell your deck how it first caught your eye, what it feels like to handle it (no blushing), and what you find most beautiful or intriguing about it. Mention what you find most challenging about it and share with it your dreams for what you'll be able to do together. Make a promise for the part you'll play.
3. When you've finished writing your letter, read it aloud to your deck. This is very important because Tarot decks can't read, but they are very good listeners.
4. You might like to sprinkle the letter with a few drops of essential oil or your favorite perfume and store it in the same box or bag as your deck. That way, every time you get your deck out, the smell will remind you of the special bond you have.

Building a Bridge

The Emperor

Every relationship is a two-way street. Your deck has needs too, which is why it's important to ask not only what your deck can do for you, but what you can do for your deck. If you don't, your deck will think you're taking advantage, and one day, you might suddenly find you're talking to yourself...

1. Shuffle the cards thoroughly, asking your deck to show you how it sees your relationship.
2. When you've finished shuffling, lay the cards out as follows.

3. After interpreting the cards, make sure you follow through. Work out how to put what you've learned into action, so your deck knows you take its needs seriously.

A: What I'm currently bringing to the relationship

Your deck knows if your heart's not really in the relationship, and will call you on it here. On the other hand, if your deck thinks you're a dedicated devotee, this card will acknowledge that.

B: What my deck brings to the relationship

This card shows what role your deck believes *it* plays in the relationship. Does it see itself as your teacher, your friend, your lover, or your pet hamster?

C: What I can do for my deck

This card shows what your deck needs from you. Read it as an advice card. Is it asking you to be more open-minded and relaxed? Or would it like you to sit up straight and stop daydreaming in class?

D: What my deck can do for me

Your deck doesn't expect you to give without getting anything in return. This card shows what gift it will bestow on you for your efforts. Keep your fingers crossed for a shiny gold star.

E: Overall advice for the relationship

This card brings the two sides together. It shows you what's most important in your relationship with your deck and the direction the relationship can take. If you feel you and your deck aren't seeing eye to eye, this card will tell you how to overcome your differences.

Voices in Your Head

The Hierophant

By now, you should be starting to understand that your deck has endless amounts of wisdom to impart. Your job is simply to sit still and pay attention. Reading Tarot is not so much about remembering what the cards mean as listening to what they say. Go on – hold a card up to your ear. Can you hear it whispering? What is it telling you?

1. Place your deck face down on the table in front of you.
2. You are going to turn each card over one by one and jot down what the people in the card are thinking or saying. Remember to jot down the name of the card as well.
3. Don't give yourself time to think about it – this will only let your own thoughts get in the way. The key to this exercise is speed.
4. If you turn over a card which doesn't have any people in it (or animals, who have a lot to say too), just go straight to the next card.
5. When you've finished with the whole deck, review what you've written. Did any of the cards surprise you?

Getting to Know You

The Lovers

The best way to get to know anyone is to ask them about themselves. Everyone loves to feel interesting. Your deck might look like it's just a stack of cardboard rectangles, but that doesn't mean it doesn't have hopes and dreams, hobbies and interests, quirks and foibles. Giving your deck the chance to share its innermost thoughts with you will let it know that you care...

1. Choose one of the questions (next page) to ask your deck or think up your own.
2. Shuffle your deck attentively, but don't let it feel self-conscious. Languidly think of the question you've asked as you shuffle, then draw one card as your deck's answer.
3. Think about the card you've drawn. What is your deck telling you about itself with this card?

Suggested Questions:

- What kind of movies do you like to watch?
- How do you like to spend your free time?
- What annoys you?
- What's your favorite time of year?
- What subject interests you most?
- If you could travel anywhere in the world, where would you like to go?
- If you could choose to have any career, what would you choose?
- What do you see as your purpose in life?
- What aspect of yourself are you most proud of?
- What do you think is your biggest flaw?
- What quality do you most admire in a person?
- How would you define true love?
- What do you believe is the meaning of life?

Taroga

The Chariot

Yoga is a centuries old discipline, the practice of which aligns body, mind, and soul in one enlightened being, allowing us to transcend the mundane and function on a higher metaphysical plane. Taroga, on the other hand, is an extremely dubious, made-up exercise of no benefit to anyone – but it does give you an excuse to play with your cards…

1. Consult your doctor before starting this program of activity if you are elderly, pregnant, perennially clumsy, drunk, bow-legged or weak-kneed, or if you are suffering from tiredness, vertigo, sea-sickness, gangrene, smelly feet, sore throat, or a common cold. NEVER attempt to perform this exercise whilst riding a bike or standing on a tightrope. The author, publisher, typesetter, and the person who sold you this book will not accept any responsibility for you falling over and hurting yourself whilst performing Taroga, so put down some cushions and don't let the dog join in.
2. Change into something floaty and preferably white. Remove your shoes, socks, ties, make–up, jewelry, hair ornaments, and mobile phone.
3. Kneel down and shuffle your cards whilst meditatively humming "ohmmmm."
4. Take the first nine cards from the top of the deck and place them face up in a row in front of you.
5. Starting with the card on the left, adopt a yoga–style pose suggested by the image on the card. Use your body to recreate the shape and form of any object on the card – it could be a person, or it could be a tree, a horse, a lobster, or a swirl of color.
6. Once you have achieved the pose, hold it for a count of ten or as long as you can without toppling over. Focus on your breathing. Listen to your heart beating. Feel the mysterious energy of the card penetrate your calf muscles.
7. Perform a yoga pose for each of the nine cards in front of you. Try to make each pose different to the last.
8. When you have completed the final pose, kneel back down and gather the cards in your hands. Thank them for enlightening you; then return them to the deck.

Split Personality

Strength

No one is straightforward – no, not even your Tarot deck. Capable of varying its mood from happy to sad and its tone of voice from gentle to stern – as the situation demands – your deck is a walking contradiction, just like any human being (except for the fact it can't walk). Use this exercise to delve into the dark recesses of your deck's psyche so you don't get any nasty surprises later on...

1. Start by shuffling your deck thoroughly so it doesn't know if it's coming or going.
2. Choose a pair of contrasting words from the list below or think up some of your own.
3. One by one, carefully analyze every card in your deck to determine which word out of the pair it most closely identifies with. As you work through the deck, sort the cards into two piles to represent each word.
4. Try not to take the words too literally or assign any kind of positive or negative connotation to either pile. There's no good or bad here – only varying expressions of the untamable individuality of your deck.

Suggested Word Pairs:

- Light / Dark
- Rich / Poor
- Hot / Cold
- Fast / Slow
- Rough / Smooth
- Open / Closed
- Moving / Still
- Big / Small
- Old / Young

Drawing Closer

The Hermit

As every great lover will tell you, real intimacy comes through knowledge. To truly appreciate your deck, you must first trace every contour and follow every line. You must feel the hilt of every sword, the throat of every cup, the rough bark of every wand and the hard curves of every pentacle. Only then will it be possible for you and your deck to become one...

1. You will need plain paper and a pencil, plus some coloring pencils, felt tips, or paints. Feel free to wear a smock and use an easel if the mood takes you.
2. Shuffle your deck and draw one card at random.
3. Trace round the card onto the paper, then carefully copy every single detail from the card inside the frame.
4. As you draw, the close attention you pay to the image and the movement of the pencil in your hand will help to cement the card in your mind's eye. You may also notice details you haven't noticed before, such as that freckle on the left shoulder of the Queen of Wands (made you look).
5. When you're satisfied you've copied the card as closely as possible, color it in. Again, try to use the same colors as the original artist. This is not forgery, it's a homage (unless you're very, very good).
6. When you've finished, you can use your version of the card as a bookmark or – if it's truly a masterpiece – hang it on your wall.

Once Upon a Time

The Wheel of Fortune

Once upon a time, in a kingdom far, far away, there was a Tarot deck that was more beautiful and more wise than anyone in the land. People traveled miles to listen to the Tarot's wondrous tales of lowly fools and impetuous knights, and would wonder at the messages hidden within the folds of each story. One day...

1. Shuffle your deck thoroughly to get a good mix of handsome princes and wicked stepmothers.
2. Place the deck face down and turn over the top card. Begin your tale by using the image on that card to complete this sentence: *Once upon a time there was...* An injured soldier? A talking cup?
3. Turn over the next card and lay it overlapping the first. Continue your story: *...who, more than anything in the world, wanted...* Something? Someone? To join the circus?
4. *But alas...* Turn over another card to find out what terrible obstacle is preventing your hero or heroine from getting what they so desire.
5. *Then one day...* Now allow the story to take over. Keep drawing cards one at a time, each one carrying the story a little bit further.
6. Keep going until you run out of ideas or cards, or until you reach a *"happily ever after"* (or a *"which is why you should never try to swallow a sword without proper training"*).
7. When you're finished with one story, shuffle the deck and start again. Or weave yourself a different bedtime story every night. Don't feel tied to the fairy tale genre – try setting your stories in the present day, in prehistoric times, in space, or wherever and whenever captures your imagination.

78 Card Soirée

Justice

Life for a Tarot deck can be all work, work, work. Throwing a party gives your deck a chance to run wild – to let its hair down, feast on some nibbles and engage in some small talk – all of which is essential for its emotional and psychological wellbeing. Watch the alcohol though: No one wants a reading from a pickled deck...

1. Go through your deck and pick out any cards which feature people (or dragons or ferrets, depending on the theme of the deck). These are your party-goers. Put the rest of the deck to one side.
2. Spread your party-goers face down on a table and swirl them around so they mingle. You might like to put on some music now – an Eighties mix-tape perhaps, or whatever you think your deck might like.
3. Choose a group of three or four cards that are touching and turn them face up. These are the first guests to arrive at your party. See what impression your party-goers make:

   • Did the card's occupants arrive alone or with party-goers from another card?
   • What kind of entrance did they make?
   • Are they happy to be there or would they rather be somewhere else?
   • How well do they get on with the other party-goers?
   • What's their behavior like?

4. Keep turning cards face up to add more guests until either the party fizzles out or the police are called to break things up.

Cliffhangers

The Hanged Man

Will Mitch finally tell Paige how he feels about her? Will Farrah admit to Greg that the baby isn't his? Will Lacey ever wake from her coma? Tune in next week to find out. Or, if you can't wait that long, just ask your cards. They know everything...

1. For this you will need a television, a pencil and paper, and a burning desire to find out what will happen in the next episode of your favorite show.
2. Get comfy and watch the current episode. When the show ends, jot down a few words for all the major storylines, e.g., Crystal and Mario's affair, Kane runs away to join the circus.
3. Shuffle your deck and draw one to three cards for each storyline.
4. Make a note of what you think each card is saying will happen to those characters. Store the piece of paper under a plant pot next to the television until the next episode is on; then use it to score your deck on its psychic abilities. Don't worry if it gets everything wrong. Some Tarot decks simply consider television to be beneath them.

All Wrapped Up

Death

They say it's better to give than to receive, but They have clearly never spent Christmas Eve at the mall trying to find that one perfect gift. If shopping for your loved ones makes you break out in a cold sweat maybe it's time to simplify. This year, why not give the gift of Tarot? Just imagine the looks on their faces as they tear the wrapping paper...

1. Jot down the names of all your loved ones, best friends, your favorite people in the whole wide world, and all those other people you have to buy gifts for.
2. For each person on the list, search your Tarot deck for one card that you would like to give them. Think carefully about which card in particular would make the perfect present for that person. Maybe choose a card that you think will inspire them or comfort them, or that captures their unique personality.
3. Remove the card from your deck, wrap it in pretty paper and give it to your loved one the very first opportunity you get.
4. Or...if the idea of giving away bits of your deck is unbearable (as it should be), try using the card to suggest an alternative gift. Ask the card, "If you were a present, what present would you be?" Then buy that instead.

The Whole Enchilada

Temperance

It may or may not be true that you can see a world in a grain of sand, but it's certainly true that you can see the whole world in a Tarot deck. Most readings only use a handful of cards, but with 78 vibrant, intelligent, fascinating images to behold, it's a shame not to let them all play together. Just be sure to mark them back in again at the end to check none have escaped...

1. Look through your deck and pick out all the Major Arcana cards. Lay them out in front of you in number order. You need to leave quite a bit of space between each card, so it's probably best to do this on the floor unless you happen to own a banqueting table.
2. Shuffle the rest of the deck.
3. Starting with the card at the top of the deck, decide which Major Arcana it is most like and place it next to that card. If, for example, you decide your 4 of Pentacles card most resembles the Sun, put it down next to the Sun card.
4. It doesn't matter what reason you have for putting two cards together. It might be that they have a similar mood or artistic style, or that the people in the cards share the same facial expression or fashion sense. Or it may be something else. As long as the match makes sense to you, it's all good.
5. If you get stuck on a card and it doesn't seem to fit with any of the Major Arcana cards, put it at the bottom of the deck and come back to it later.
6. After you've assigned all of the cards, look at each Major Arcana card and the cards you matched with it. What makes each clique unique? Consider giving each group a nickname – in fact, why stop there? Arrange for each group to meet up once a week to give the cards a sense of belonging and camaraderie. When the "Charioteers" start pouring slushies over the "Tea and Temperancers," you'll know you've done a good thing.

Build Your Own Superhero

The Devil

Oh no! A beautiful blonde is plummeting from a skyscraper and a bus load of schoolchildren is teetering off a bridge and a frail old lady is being mugged by a masked thug and a nerdy, bespectacled man is trapped inside a phone booth! Who will save them? Why, SuperTarot of course!

1. Hum the theme from *Superman* as you shuffle your deck, until it swells with a heroic sense of duty.
2. Arrange the top four cards face down in front of you in a diamond formation.
3. Turn over the card at the top of the diamond. This card reveals your superhero's incredible superpower. Can they leap great heights? Explode things with their mind? Hop like a frog, like, really fast? Use your own super imagination to translate the image on the card into your hero's greatest strength and maybe also to suggest their superhero name.
4. Now turn over the card on the left. This reveals your superhero's secret vulnerability, their Achilles kryptonite if you will. What turns their bulging muscles to jelly and leaves them cowering in a corner crying for their mummy? What weakness would they like to keep hidden from their enemies? This card knows.
5. Talking of enemies...turn over the card on the right. This is your superhero's nemesis, the bad to his good, the dark to his light, the mongoose to his snake. Every superhero needs one really despicable archvillain to fight, so try to suck as much malevolence out of this card as you can (then rinse your mouth out with soapy water).
6. Finally, turn over the card at the bottom. This card illustrates your superhero's special superhero costume – from the colors to the cut, even down to the emblem blazing proudly on their chest. Take all that is strong and good and brave from the card and style it into a second skin worthy of the greatest crime fighter in the world.
7. Now that you've created a brave new superhero, you can make it your alter ego and practice your moves in your bedroom when no one's looking. Or, you can shuffle the deck and get on with your real life.

Cryptarotography

The Tower

Tarot is a symbolic language. A bird is never simply a bird. A stone is never simply a stone. No Tarotist would ever dare call a spade a spade (as it's clearly a sword). Hermetic occultists have spent lifetimes coding and decoding this most sacred and esoteric of alphabets. Fortunately for you, this piece of encryption should take less than an hour…

1. You will need something to write on and something to write with. The "on" should be crisp and white, and the "with" should be sharpened to an atom-sized point.
2. List the card names down the left-hand-side of the paper. Though this be a menial task, do not let your mind wander or you'll miss one out and have to start all over again.
3. Place all the cards in a face-down pile. It doesn't matter what order they're in, although the order in which the artist painted them would be ideal.
4. Turn the top card over. Study it for a symbol or detail that you believe is unique to that card. Look for something distinctive and easy to recall. It also helps if it's something quite central to the image – an arched window is good, a broken toenail is not.
5. When you've chosen, make a simplified drawing of that object next to the card's name in the list. Imagine you are creating a hieroglyph – it should be a true copy of the original item but it should also possess a certain economy of style, making it easy to replicate. For example, if you've chosen a feather, you might draw one long curved line dissected by several shorter lines (this could also be used to represent a kebab).
6. Do the same for every card in the deck.
7. When you've finished, store your list of codes in a safe place. It is your personal Rosetta Stone. Use these codes any time you wish to journal a reading that is particularly personal (or to thwart your nosy little sister). Or, for even more fun and giggles, share your code with a close friend and use it whenever you do readings for each other.

Scratch and Sniff

The Star

When you look at your cards, what do you hear? They say Tarot is a visual medium, but in truth it can be so much more. Not just a pretty face, your deck is bursting with enough sounds, tastes, smells, and textures to turn every reading into a carnival. Which explains why the Wheel of Fortune sounds like a merry-go-round and the Page of Wands stinks of hot dogs...

1. Shuffle your deck and turn over the top card.
2. Using the image as a cue, try to figure out what sound the card reminds you of. For example, you might associate the 9 of Wands with the sound of soldiers trudging through mud or Gloria Gaynor's "I Will Survive." Try to tune in to the unique sound of your particular card.
3. Now decide what the card smells like. The Empress might smell of a fragrant garden but the Hermit isn't known for his personal hygiene and could very well smell of mold.
4. Next, focus on your fingertips and your sense of touch. Look at the scene depicted in the card – the colors, the textures, the location, and the people. Remember that touch can sense hot and cold, hard and soft, rough and smooth, sharp and blunt. Work out what your card makes you feel. The 8 of Pentacles might feel like heavy, oily machinery while the Queen of Pentacles might feel like luxurious velvet drapes.
5. Finally, smack your lips together and try to taste the card. The Moon may be made of cheese but sometimes it tastes like absinthe. Don't limit yourself to food and drink flavors either. If you think the Devil tastes like fetid cowpats, say so (just don't say it to his face).
6. Repeat for each card in the deck, or until you collapse from sensory overload.

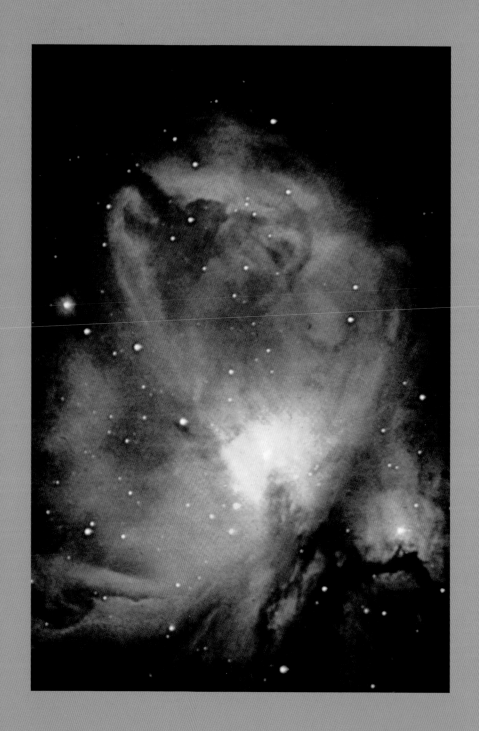

Little White Book

The Moon

Most Tarot decks come with a *Little White Book* (LWB) – a folded piece of paper containing brief and enigmatic divinatory meanings for each card. Notorious for being about as useful as a sponge submarine, this LWB is nonetheless the only thing you can fall back on when you get stuck. Or is it? If you're going to consult confusing riddles, shouldn't they at least be *your* confusing riddles?

1. Shuffle your deck and draw a card at random.
2. Try to ignore any "standard" meanings that pop into your head: These are of no use in an LWB. Allow your vision to blur slightly, try tilting your head to one side, and move the card as close to your face as possible. Now what do you see?
3. Translate your findings into a short and profoundly meaningless sentence. For example, "Paths converge, a stranger beckons, purple orchids never lie."
4. Repeat steps 1–3 for each card in the deck.
5. You may like to keep a record of your deck's new "suggested divinatory elucidations" by creating a new LWB. Use a folded sheet of A4 paper so you can store it with your cards, and be sure to use very, very tiny handwriting.

Whodunit

The Sun

A crime has been committed – a most heinous murder! One of the court cards is responsible, but which one? Before you jump to conclusions and throw the Knight of Swords in jail, it's perhaps wise to examine the evidence. You need to uncover not just whodunit, but how and why. It's time to gather everyone in the drawing room...

1. Divide the deck into three separate piles of Major Arcana cards, aces, and Minor Arcana cards. Remove the Death card from the Major Arcana cards then shuffle each pile.
2. Spread the court cards out so you can see each one. Keep a close eye on them at all times. They're all suspects and they're all guilty until proven innocent.
3. As there's been a murder, there must be a body. Turn over the top card of the Major Arcana pile. If it has a person on it, that's your victim. (If it hasn't, try again.) Give the victim a name to humanize them and make their death seem all the more tragic. For example, Ira Fant might make a good name for a priest.
4. Next, find the murder weapon. Don forensic examination gloves and turn over the top card of the aces pile.

   - The Ace of Cups means your victim was poisoned.
   - The Ace of Swords means they were stabbed.
   - The Ace of Wands means they were shot.
   - The Ace of Pentacles means they were hit over the head with something heavy (an enormous coin perhaps).

5. Now you can round up everyone who had the means to commit this murder – that is, all the court cards that had access to the murder weapon. So if the victim was poisoned, you need to track down all four Cups court cards. Place these prime suspects side-by-side in a police line-up. Pay attention to anyone who looks particularly shifty.
6. Next, question each of the suspects to discover their motives. Adopt a "bad cop" attitude and interrogate each court. Turn over one Minor Arcana card for each suspect and study the image to

uncover why they would want the victim dead. Be thorough – any minor detail could be a clue to their motive!

7. Finally, it's time to unmask the killer. Return the Death card to the Major Arcana pile and shuffle well. Shoot intimidating glances at the prime suspects as you do so. Then, starting with the left-most court card, deal the Major Arcana cards out one by one on top of the suspects. Whoever gets dealt the Death card is the murderer!

A Present for the Future

Judgement

How will we use Tarot in the future? Will we shuffle holographic decks? Will the astral plane travel at the speed of light? Will we foretell of meetings with little green men instead of tall dark strangers? If only we had some means of finding out...

1. Shuffle your cards at exactly 88 miles per hour.
2. As you shuffle, project your mind forward one year, to the (insert today's date) of (insert current month), (insert this year + 1). Ask your cards to show you that day.
3. Draw three cards and place them in front of you.
4. The first card gives you a glimpse of the FUTURE YOU – who you will be or what you will be doing exactly one year from now.
5. The second card reveals your FIGHT IN THE FUTURE – the main obstacle you will be struggling against on the specified day.
6. The last card shows your WISDOM OF THE AGES – this will be the wise voice from the past that helps you overcome your future challenge.
7. After you've drawn the cards, find a piece of paper and jot down today's date, the name of your deck, and which cards you drew in each position. Write one line about what you think each of the cards is showing you. Fold the paper and write the future date on the outside then carefully store it in a safe yet totally memorable location.
8. In one year's time, retrieve the gift your past self left for your future (present) self. Swoon in amazement at the accuracy of your prediction. Weep with gratitude at the timeliness of the advice.
9. If you suffer from extreme impatience, try reading ahead one month or one week. Though be warned, it's not as likely you'll encounter little green men.

Through the Peephole

The World

The first weeks and months that you spend getting to know your cards are crucial – a time when bonds of friendship, trust, and intimacy are formed. During this period, it's vital that you don't do anything that will jeopardize the fragile and beautiful relationship that is blossoming. For example, spying on your cards is a definite no-no...

1. You need some stiff card stock paper. Any color will do, but black will create that authentic covert ops feel.
2. Trace and cut out a piece of card stock paper the same size and shape as your Tarot cards. Using a small coin as a template (approximately 1–2 cm in diameter), draw and cut out a circular peephole anywhere on the card. From now on, this advanced piece of technology shall be known as the Tarotscope.
3. Shuffle your deck. Talk to it casually about mundane affairs so it doesn't suspect what you're up to.
4. When you've finished shuffling, place the deck face down in front of you and close your eyes. Turn over the top card and place the Tarotscope over the card, making sure the whole card is covered.
5. Open your eyes and try to identify the card by what's visible through the hole in the Tarotscope. When you think you know what it is (or you give up in frustration) remove the Tarotscope to uncover the card's true identity.
6. Perform this secret maneuver whenever your deck's guard is down, but be sure to never get caught.

The Sound of Silence

Ace of Wands

Long periods of silence are a true test of any relationship. Sure, you and your deck get on fine at the movies or window shopping at a busy mall, but can you spend an evening together without talking, switching on the TV, or whistling annoying jingles? If you can, there's hope for you yet...

1. Retreat to a tranquil part of your house – or seek out a quiet glade in some distant wood where there is no one to hear if a tree falls.
2. Before you begin your silent vigil, take a moment to empty yourself of noise. Clear your throat. Cough. Hum. Sing a few scales in B flat minor. Shout. Scream. Beat your chest.
3. And relax...
4. Now shuffle your deck. As you do, let the day's stresses leave you. Allow silence to settle on you like snowflakes falling on a deserted beach. Gradually slow your shuffling until you are cradling your deck in your hands.
5. As quietly as possible, turn the top card over and place it in front of you. Say nothing. If possible, think nothing.
6. Take the next card and place it beside the first. Be as quiet as a daffodil.
7. Turn over a third card and lay it next to the other cards. Hush...
8. Continue in this fashion until you are surrounded by cards. Do not stare at them but merely sit with them, in silence, for as long as you can manage. Listen to them breathe. Watch a sunlit dust mote float down onto the Emperor's nose. Be idle. Laze. Do not text your friends.
9. When you grow fidgety and can't take the silence anymore, jump up and gather your cards, dancing and singing at the top of your voice.
10. Repeat this exercise whenever you feel you and your cards have spent more time doing than being, or when you need an excuse to get out of a boring social engagement.

A Rose By Any Other

2 of Wands

Now that you and your deck have spent some quality time together, you're hopefully starting to feel ready to move your relationship to the next level. But before you do, isn't it about time you stopped addressing your deck by its full name? "The Tarot of the Inflated Ego" might be fine for black tie functions and the taxman, but your new pal deserves something far more warm and fuzzy...

1. Spread out some of your favorite cards from your deck for inspiration.
2. Think for a few minutes about the unique qualities of your deck. If you were to describe it to someone who'd never seen it before, what sort of words would you use? Jot down a few adjectives that you feel best capture your deck's personality.
3. When you can't think of any more words, choose your favorites and play with different combinations until you come up with a fabulous new name for your deck. Don't forget to ask your deck if it approves of its new name.
4. Refer to your deck by its new name whenever you're in the company of other Tarotists, to see how many of them pretend to know what you're talking about.

Part Two

Stepping Out

14 Ways to Mingle With the Minors

Eyewitness

3 of Wands

Close your eyes. Now, what do you see? If your answer is "nothing" then congratulations – your powers of perception are at their optimum level. You can now attempt the following test.

1. Shuffle the Minor Arcana until each card is well and truly lost in the crowd.
2. Deal 5 cards face up in a cloud shape, so they're touching and jostling each other for space.
3. Study the cards for 30 seconds. Then scoop them up and put them to one side, face down.
4. Now, recall the people that you saw in those cards in as much detail as you can. Imagine you're being questioned by a detective and your description is crucial to busting an underground crime syndicate. Describe what they were wearing and what they were carrying. Give their eye and hair color. What about height and build? Is there anything else you can think of – anything at all? Jot it all down for the record.
5. When you've finished giving your statement, take a look at the cards again to check your accuracy. Would the police be able to identify the suspects based on the information you provided? If so, give yourself a pat on the back and a cash reward. If not, tell yourself that eyewitness accounts are notoriously unreliable and besides, shouldn't the police be out doing some real detective work instead of counting on the testimony of someone who clearly doesn't know what they're talking about? Exactly.

Literal Thinking

4 of Wands

Reading Tarot: It's all about intuition, isn't it? Using your imagination, reading between the lines, listening to your inner moonbeam – all these things can make you a better reader. But sometimes the universe likes to have a little joke. Sometimes the cards say exactly what they mean, leaving you feeling like someone about to walk off a cliff...

1. This is best attempted early in the morning, preferably when you've just woken up and think you're still dreaming.
2. Shuffle the Minor Arcana. As you do so, recite the following lines:

    Tell an owl toowit–toowoo
    And she'll reply toowit–toowee
    So show me clear and show me true
    What peril is in store for me!

3. Stop shuffling and take the bottom-most card. Put the other cards aside.
4. Focus your attention on the card. Imagine it's a road sign, warning you of danger ahead. What is it telling you to look out for today? Keep it simple and stick to what the card shows. No traditional meanings or intuitive psychic flashes are allowed. For example, the Tower card might mean beware of falling kings and the 6 of Cups might tell you to be suspicious of children bearing gifts.
5. Keep the card's message in mind throughout the day. Congratulate yourself if you make it to bed at night without suffering any mishaps (unless you drew the 9 of Swords, in which case it's probably best not to go to bed at all).

Rain or Shine

5 of Wands

There's nothing in life more frustrating than the weather. Just when you think you've got everything under control, a freak snow storm ruins your new suede shoes or you're caught out in a heat wave wearing a balaclava. Fortunately, Tarot can save the day. Put your deck to work forecasting the weather and you'll never be inappropriately dressed again (for the weather, that is...)

1. First, perform the weather forecasting ritual. Dress in raincoat, sunglasses, woolen gloves and Wellington boots. Go outside and place the Minor Arcana cards on the ground in the shade of an umbrella then hold your hands up to the heavens whilst chanting:

   Whether shine or whether rain,
   Make mine cards a weather vane!

2. Remove your gloves and shuffle the cards until dark clouds gather overhead. (If no dark clouds form, you may continue, but the ritual will not be as powerful as it could be.)
3. Take the top five cards and lay them out in a row. These cards forecast the weather for the following day.

   - Wands predict sunshine
   - Cups are rain
   - Swords indicate wind
   - Pentacles represent snow, hail and other solid precipitation such as frogs

4. Refer to the card numbers to forecast the intensity of the weather system. For example, the Ace of Cups probably suggests a light shower whereas the 10 of Swords could predict a cyclone.
5. Read the cards in sequence to predict how the weather will change throughout the day. Look for further clues in the cards to add the kind of specific predictive details that will really impress your friends. For example, "There will be a light north-easterly wind that will stir up some leaves and cause your knife to be blown from your hand as you're eating dinner."

6. Once your forecast has been made, the dark clouds should recede. Shuffle the cards back in with the rest of the Minor Arcana and retreat indoors. If you like, turn on the TV to check if the "real" weather forecasters have got it right.

Making Headlines

6 of Wands

Every journalist knows the six essential ingredients that make a news story: Who, What, When, Where, How, and Why. They also know that anything can be newsworthy if you find the right angle. You've just got to sniff out the story, dig up some dirt, and voila! Suddenly, the chess club is a den of iniquity and the vicar's wife is a closet dominatrix...

1. The aim of this game is to try to predict the top story on the front of tomorrow's newspaper. Decide now which newspaper you're going to tune in on.
2. Shuffle the Minor Arcana cards thoroughly. As you do so, adopt a serious yet reassuring countenance. If possible, sit behind a desk and wear a suit.
3. Stop shuffling when your cards have grasped the gravity of the situation, and lay the top six cards face down in front of you.
4. Turn over the first card. This card reveals WHO the news story is about. Is it one person or many? Male or female? Young or old? What is their profession?
5. Turn over the second card. This is WHAT the news story is about – in a nutshell, what happens. What does the card show? Is it a fight, a discovery, a death, or the birth of a baby panda?
6. Turn over the third card which represents WHEN the story happens. Does this card suggest something that is over and done with, or something that is in progress? Are there any clues in the card to suggest the time of day?
7. Turn over the fourth card. This card shows WHERE the news story happens. Is it inside or outside? Busy or quiet? Does the activity in the card suggest a certain type of place? Run through some possibilities in your mind to see which best fits the story so far.
8. Turn over the fifth card to find out HOW the event happens. Think of this card as providing the flavor of the piece. Is there jubilation or is there chaos and panic? Is it all dry, boring financial talk or a breezy piece of celebrity gossip?

9. Turn over the sixth card to shed some light on WHY it all happens. What led to this event? What is at the root of the story? This card may reveal the motive for a crime or simply the deep dark secret that a politician is trying to hide.

10. Finally, put it all together. Shuffle some papers and clear your throat. Say, "Good evening, and here is the news." Then read your news story. When tomorrow comes (or *if* tomorrow comes, in the event that your story predicts Armageddon), check it against the headlines to see how you did.

Two Become One

7 of Wands

In this futuristic age of genetic engineering, clones, robotics, and intelligent toasters, the idea of pictures printed on cardboard seems rather quaint. What better way to drag your Tarot deck into the 21st Century than to subject it to some gene splicing? Mutant Tarot cards of the world unite!

1. Shuffle the Minor Arcana and ask for two volunteers to take part in an experiment. If no cards step forward, pick two at random. Name them Subject A and Subject B.
2. Lay the two cards side by side and examine each one's dominant traits. What stands out in each card? What symbolic features and colors seem most important?
3. Using tracing paper, copy the main elements of each card and transfer them to plain paper. Try to trace several items from each card to get a varied gene pool. Cut them out.
4. On a new sheet of paper, draw around one of the cards as a template. Assemble the pieces you've cut out inside the frame to create a new card – the love child, if you will, of Subject A and Subject B. Glue the pieces down when you're happy with your creation.
5. Use pencils, crayons, felt tips, or paints to color in Subject C. Use colors that are common to both Subject A and Subject B or combine those cards' dominant colors. Cut the card out when you've finished.
6. As with any new addition to the family, you should name Subject C. Give it both an official name and a nickname. For example, the offspring of the 4 of Pentacles and the 2 of Cups might officially be known as the 6 of Pentacups (or Cupsacles)! For the nickname, consider the personality of your new card and how it makes you feel. What keyword or title might suit the card? Write both names on the card.
7. Integrate the card with the rest of your deck to confound your Tarot reading friends.

Remember Remember

8 of Wands

Feed the cat, wash the car, take Grandma to have her hair done, order a new iron. Feed Grandma, take the cat to have her hair done, wash the iron, order a new car. Take the iron to Grandma's, feed the car, order a new cat — do you have trouble keeping track of things? If so, this should almost certainly confuse you further...

1. Make a list of everything you need to do today.
2. Shuffle the Minor Arcana.
3. Try to remember where you put the list you just made.
4. Select one card from your deck for each "to do" item on your list. The card should contain some visual clue related to what you have to do so it will help you remember. For example, Death may be a good card to remind you to mow the lawn (but only if you own a large scythe).
5. Once you have chosen a card for each task, tear up your list and throw it away (or, better yet, recycle it). You should have no need for such a lowly mnemonic device now that you have Tarot cards.
6. Keep your Cards of Remembering in your bag or pocket and carry them around with you all day. Remember to check them to see what it is you're supposed to be doing. Remember to return them to your Tarot deck when you've finished with them. And remember to put Grandma out before you go to bed.

About Time

9 of Wands

How good is your deck's sense of timing? Could you set your watch by it? Some decks are so tightly wound that every card knows its place in the schedule. Other decks are more laid back and about as punctual as the Fool on his day off. If your deck is chronologically challenged, don't worry; use this activity to get it to fall in line...

1. Go outside and draw a large chalk circle on the ground or, if you prefer to work indoors, mark out a circle on the floor using something small, cheap and consumable. Dried pasta is good.
2. Make a mark at each 90° point around the circle beginning at the top. Label the top of the circle "midnight" and the bottom of the circle "midday." On the right–hand mark write "6am" and on the opposite side write "6pm." If you're not using chalk, mark each of these points with different objects which suggest those times. For example, use a boiled egg for the morning and a dry martini for the evening.
3. Shuffle the Minor Arcana cards and place them face down in the center of the circle.
4. Turn over the top card and study the image. Look for clues in the image that relate to time of day. It could be anything: If the moon or sun is depicted, that will of course indicate day or night but try to be even more specific than that. Think what time of day the colors, symbols and scenes on the card suggest. For example, a card showing travelers setting out on a journey might evoke early morning and one that is predominantly purple-gray in color might conjure up visions of late evening.
5. Place the card at the appropriate place on the circle-clock; then do the same for every card in the pile. Feel free to make adjustments to the position of any card as you progress.
6. When you've finished, take a look at the placement of the cards to see what it tells you about your deck. Are the cards spread out evenly around the circle suggesting a well-balanced deck? Or are they all clumped around midnight, suggesting your deck is nocturnal and secretive with vampiric tendencies?

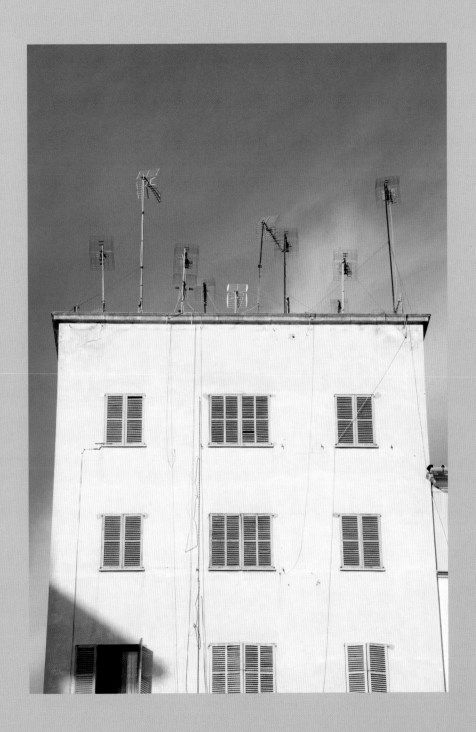

Wishful Thinking

10 of Wands

Don't wish upon a star – everyone does that. Make your wishes really special by wishing on those most powerful of Tarot cards, the Aces. Whether it's true love you seek, or a shiny new car, the Aces can make all your dreams come true. But only if you ask them nicely and only if they feel like it.

1. Wait for a full moon.
2. Before you begin, it's a good idea to test the strength of your wishing power. Close your eyes and wish for all four aces to separate themselves from the pack and appear in your hand.
3. Open your eyes. If your wish has not been granted, this means your wishing power is extremely weak. For future wishes, use the wish enhancement modifications below. In the meantime, search the deck yourself for the aces. Place them face up in front of you and put the rest of the cards to one side.
4. Now you must decide what you want to wish for. If you already know, great. Proceed to step 5. If not, take a moment now to ponder what would make you happy. (Note: In these circumstances, it is considered impolite to wish for a new Tarot deck.)
5. Once you've settled on a wish, select the ace that governs the general area of your wish. For example, if your wish concerns money, the Ace of Pentacles is probably your best bet. Remove all the other aces from your sight so as not to contaminate the wishing process.

6. Now, lay your chosen ace in the palm of your left hand and cover it with the palm of your right hand. Close your eyes and recite the words of wishing:

Ace of wonder, manifest
The thing I ask of you,
Listen now to my request
And make my dreams come true.

7. Then – either out loud or in your head – make your wish.
8. If you performed the wish-making ceremony correctly, you should expect your wish to be granted come the next full moon. If your wish is not granted, you clearly asked for something you're not allowed to have. Do not bother the aces with the same request again.

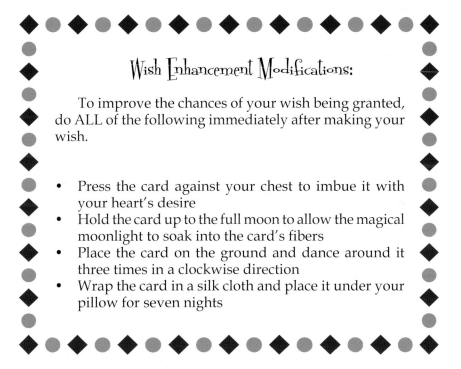

Wish Enhancement Modifications:

To improve the chances of your wish being granted, do ALL of the following immediately after making your wish.

- Press the card against your chest to imbue it with your heart's desire
- Hold the card up to the full moon to allow the magical moonlight to soak into the card's fibers
- Place the card on the ground and dance around it three times in a clockwise direction
- Wrap the card in a silk cloth and place it under your pillow for seven nights

Excuse Me

Page of Wands

Apparently there are "50 ways to leave your lover," 49 of which you should only need to know if you don't do it right the first time. However, if you find yourself short on ideas, you can always count on Tarot to come up trumps. Not only is it always full of bright ideas, it also frees you of any decision-making responsibility, which may come in handy when your angry Ex catches up with you...

1. This requires a lot of quick-thinking, so shuffle the Minor Arcana cards until they're completely wired and sparks are flying.
2. As you're shuffling (or before, or after) choose one of the themes from the list below or use whatever tricky situation you're currently trying to weasel out of.
3. Place the cards face down in front of you then with pen and paper poised, turn over the top card.
4. As quickly as possible, write down a way in which the card illustrates the theme. For example, if you chose Ways to Leave Your Lover, you might write "fake your own death" for the 10 of Swords.
5. As soon as you've jotted something down for that card, move onto the next. See if you can come up with an idea for every one of the 40 Minor Arcana cards.
6. When you've finished, fold the paper and put it in your pocket. Next time you find yourself in a sticky situation, you'll have no shortage of excuses to get you out of it.

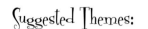

Suggested Themes:

- Ways to leave your lover
- Excuses for why you couldn't make it into work today
- Reasons why it was necessary for you to drive at twice the speed limit
- Reasons why your best friend has to lend you a lot of money
- Explanations for what is going on when your partner catches you in a compromising position with someone else
- Reasons why you absolutely positively had to eat the last chocolate in the box

Stealing the Scene

Knight of Wands

Did you know that Tarot cards can freeze time? It's true – doing a Tarot reading is like taking a snapshot of a situation; it allows you to take a good hard look to see what's really going on. But what would happen if you created your own snapshot? Choose the players, set the scene, then watch the drama unfold...

1. To begin, pick a theme from the list below. Or, if you can think of a better idea, use that.
2. Spread the Minor Arcana cards out so you can see every card.
3. Start with the centerpiece of your scene. If you opted for a wedding, you'll first need to find your happy couple. Similarly, if you chose to stage a funeral you'll need a corpse. If there isn't one card that can act as a centerpiece on its own, try putting two or more cards side by side.
4. Now look for cards to depict the other key elements of your scene. For example, at a traditional wedding you might find: a vicar or registrar, the best man, the father of the bride, bridesmaids, several wedding guests (some tipsy), a photographer, a wedding planner, and lots and lots of flowers. Again, feel free to combine cards to create the desired effect.
5. When you've found the cards you want to use, you need to decide where to put them. Consider the overall picture you're creating. Imagine your tableau to be like a photograph of the event and arrange your players accordingly.
6. Don't be afraid to break with tradition. So the bride and groom are setting off on their honeymoon in a rowing boat across a misty lake? How romantic!
7. When you've finished setting up the scene, take a closer look at the cards. What stories are hidden in the combinations you've chosen? What sordid secrets are hinted at in the body language and facial expressions? What's that you say? The mother of the bride is taking bets on how long it lasts? Shame on her!

Suggested Scenes:

- A wedding
- A funeral
- Celebrating the birth of a baby
- A glamorous awards ceremony
- A major sporting event, such as a boxing match or a horse race
- A court case in action
- Daylight robbery
- Love at first sight
- The good Samaritan

Knock Knock

Queen of Wands

As everyone knows, Tarot cards are very spooky and are mainly used for communicating with the Other Side – which makes them ideal for contacting the spirits that haunt the Minor Arcana. Now remember: One knock means *yes* and two means *no*. Or was that the other way round?

1. You will need a circular table and a tablecloth with a long fringe.
2. Sit at the table and shuffle the Minor Arcana cards until you stir up all the spectral energy in the deck. Place the cards face down on the table in front of you.
3. Place your hands on the table with your palms up and close your eyes. Imagine the cards levitating and swirling in the air before you, rearranging themselves as desired by the attendant spirits. Open your eyes once the cards have settled back down into a neat pile.
4. Now, circle the table in a clockwise direction, dealing the cards into eight piles of five, as though you were laying place settings for eight dinner guests.
5. When you've finished laying the cards, stand at the head of the table and recite the following:

   Knock, knock, who's there?
   Come in, pull up a chair.
   Tell me now what bothers you
   And I will tell you what to do.

6. If a real ghost should appear, feel free to run screaming from the room as that isn't supposed to happen. What *should* happen is that you're drawn to one of the eight piles of cards. Lay those cards in a row in the center of the table. Interpret the cards to find out how you can heal their paranormal pain.
7. The first card is the TROUBLED SOUL that needs your help. Who were they when they were alive? What happened to them?
8. The second card shows you AN ITEM THEY'VE LOST. Why is this item so important to them? Why are they so desperate to get it back?

9. The third card shows some UNFINISHED BUSINESS they have in this world. Apart from finding the item they've lost, what wrong are they seeking to right? What message do they need to impart?
10. The fourth card tells you HOW THEY CAN FIND what they've lost. What should they do or where should they look?
11. Use the fifth card to give them CLOSURE in their worldly woes – even if it's too late to put things right you can help them find peace.
12. By the time you've finished, the restless spirit should be ready to move on. Remember to cover your eyes so you're not blinded by the white light that welcomes them into the next realm.

The Devil Danced Decadently

King of Wands

We all know it's not what you do, it's the way that you do it, which is to say, there's a world of difference between a warrior resting wearily and a warrior resting permanently. (Or maybe there's just a *word* of difference, the author chuckled wryly.) Adverbs are the color–commentary of any sentence, as this game vigorously demonstrates...

1. Shuffle the Minor Arcana cards languorously.
2. Decisively cut the cards into three face-down piles excitedly.
3. Turn over the top card of each pile mysteriously. Arrange all three cards face-up in a row hypnotically.
4. Observe the first card maniacally to find the subject of your sentence – who or what the card shows. Write down the name of the subject triumphantly, for example, "The Peasant," "The Warrior," or "The Cup."
5. Behold the second card ponderously and endearingly write down the verb it suggests, for example, "fought," "jumped," or "chiseled." Look deeply for the action that is shown in the image.
6. Heroically study the third card to uncover the adverb of your sentence, for example, "explosively," "glamorously," or "furtively." Write it down secretly. You may fortuitously find some examples of other adverbs on this page.
7. When you've finished, read your sentence melodically then rest on your laurels smugly. Then meekly turn over a new set of cards and boisterously do it all again.

In the Mood

Ace of Cups

How we feel seriously affects how successful we are in many situations. It doesn't matter whether you're charged with fiery enthusiasm, mellow and full of love, pointy sharp and focused, or firmly rooted in the ground – if your attitude isn't in sync with the task at hand, it means you're likely to struggle. But if you let your cards get you in the right mood, suddenly anything is possible...

1. First, decide how you would like to feel. For example, if you're angry, you might want to feel more calm. And if you're about to stand in front of a hundred people singing "Copacabana" in a hot pink bikini, you might like to boost your confidence (or skip town). If you feel fine and you just want to play with your cards, pick a feeling from the Mood Directory at the end of this section. It's bound to come in handy later on.
2. Spread all the Minor Arcana cards out on the floor or a large table so you can see them all at once.
3. Pick all the cards that convey – either through color, pattern, or body language – the feeling you're seeking. Don't worry about what suit they're from: A particular Wands card might be as soothing as a Cups card, and a certain Cups card might make you feel as energized as a Wand. Focus only on the card images and the feelings they evoke for you.
4. Gather all your chosen cards together and put the rest aside. Arrange your selections in a closely packed grid so as to combine their energies and strengthen their mood-changing powers.
5. Sit in front of the cards and make yourself comfortable. Study them. Imagine they're giving off energy like flowers give off scent. Breathe it in through your nose and mouth. Imagine this energy is the feeling you crave. Imagine it flowing through your body – from your airways into your lungs and then into your bloodstream. Feel it imbuing you with raw emotion.
6. Carry the cards with you whenever you think you might need to quickly change your mood. Or photograph all the different grids you make to create a go-anywhere Mood-Modifying Flick Book™.

The Mood Directory

Happy	Melancholy	Calm	Loving
Assertive	Romantic	Patient	Strong
Focused	Playful	Confident	Dynamic
Creative	Dreamy	Authoritative	Practical
Adventurous	Diligent	Vibrant	Persuasive
Sociable	Contemplative	Generous	Flexible
Capable	Caring	Receptive	Diplomatic
Serious	Sensual	Relaxed	Defensive

E.S.P.

2 of Cups

A good measure of any relationship is how in sync two individuals are. Can you read your deck's mind? Do you finish each other's sentences? If you stub your toe, does your deck wince in pain? It's time to put your psychic link to the test…

1. Shuffle the Minor Arcana cards thoroughly and place them face down in front of you.
2. Without peeking, take the top card and place it face down in the middle of a table in an empty room. Clear all other objects from the table to avoid unwanted interference.
3. Remove yourself from the room so that you cannot see the card. Sit on an uncomfortable chair with both feet on the floor and both hands resting nonchalantly in your lap.
4. Close your eyes and slow your breathing. Visualize the face down card on the table. Take your time and try to make the image in your mind as vivid as possible. Do not think of an elephant.
5. Now picture your hand moving slowly towards the card. See your index finger and thumb gently pinching one corner. Turn it right side up.
6. Focus on the card in your mind's eye. Do you instantly recognize it as one of your Minor Arcana cards or is the image too fuzzy? Try to make out what you can. Do you see any Wands, Cups, Swords or Pentacles? If so, try to count them. Memorize any parts of the image that stand out – such as a person, a pool of water, or a giant rabbit.
7. Open your eyes and quickly jot down what you saw before you forget it. Then walk to the room where the card is. Go straight to the room without delay. Do Not Pass Go. Do Not Collect $200. Fragments of your subconscious may still be lurking there and you must reunite them with the rest of your mind as quickly as possible.
8. Now turn the card over for real. (You may like to start a drum roll before you do so.)
9. Award yourself one E.S.P. (Extra Sensory Point) if you correctly guessed the suit, and two E.S.P.s if you guessed both the suit and the card number. One bonus E.S.P. can be added for every visual detail you correctly identified. Look up your score below to find out how well you did.

The E.S.P. Key

0	Hmmm… Were you thinking of an elephant the whole time? Try again.
1	Not bad, but maybe you just got lucky. Try again.
2	Impressive. You got lucky twice. Consider moving to Las Vegas to become a professional gambler.
3	Congratulations! You and your deck are in sync. Keep practicing to strengthen your bond.
4	Wow. Pick your jaw from the floor and consider a career as a stage magician.
5+	The force is strong in this one. Call the Society for Psychical Research – they'll be expecting you.

Part Three

Friends in High Places

16 Ways to Click With the Courts

Tom, Dick, or Harry

3 of Cups

It's human nature to want to name things. We name our pets, our teddy bears, even our...cars. Giving something a name helps to define it and makes it more personal. Here's how to turn a two–dimensional Page of Wands into a fully rounded individual named Bob.

1. Focus on one court card at a time – that way, you won't overload your brain.
2. Think about the court's background. Are they male or female, young or old? Do they belong to the modern day or some historical time? If the deck has a particular theme, what sort of name would fit in with that theme?
3. Run through possible names in your head until you find one that suits the court. Don't move on to the next card until you've come up with a name you're happy with. Don't worry if you can't think of a name straight away – sometimes the perfect name will pop into your head instantly; other times, it could take several minutes (or maybe even days).
4. Remember, these names are just for you so they can be as sensible or as silly as you like. If you want to call the King of Cups Mr. Squidgy Woo–Woo, that's between you and your cards.
5. Once you've thought of names for all your court cards, take time to memorize them. Greet them by their new names whenever you cross paths and you'll soon feel like old friends.

The Great Pretender

4 of Cups

The King of Cups was immensely pleased with himself. Wishing to understand his subjects better, he had disguised himself as a travelling merchant and blended in seamlessly with village life. "Not one of them suspects that I am their Great King," he thought triumphantly. But alas, upon returning to the palace that night, he discovered he was still wearing his crown...

1. During our lives, we each have to wear many different hats. Draw 16 hat shapes on a piece of plain paper and write a profession on each hat listed on facing page.

2. Cut out the hats and fold each one in half. Find a real hat and put them all in it.

3. Hold the court cards over your head and shuffle them with your eyes closed. When you drop a card, stop shuffling and place the dropped card face up in front of you.

4. Now close your eyes again and draw a hat from the hat. Unfold it and place it on the court's head.

5. Imagine the court had to adopt the position written on the hat. How would they perform that role? Would they enjoy it? Would the role suit them or would they feel uncomfortable doing it? Think of the different tasks the job might involve and picture the court carrying them out. How would they relate to the people they had contact with? How would those people react to them?

6. When the court begins to look stressed, try them with a different hat. Try to remember which hat(s) suited them and which didn't.

7. Go through all the court cards, allowing each one to try on all the hats until they find the one they're most comfortable with. And if a particular hat seems to be the perfect fit, decorate it in their personal style and keep it close to your deck so they can try it on whenever they fancy.

Suggested Hats:

- Chef
- Racing car driver
- Primary school teacher
- Air traffic controller
- Prison guard
- Movie star
- Vet
- Dog trainer
- Tour guide
- Army drill sergeant
- Shop assistant
- Police officer
- Concierge
- Self-help guru
- Film director
- Gardener
- Driving instructor
- Fighter pilot
- Farmer
- Nurse

Common People

5 of Cups

One way to get to know your court cards is to identify all the ways in which they're different. But of course, that would be too simple. If you really want to become enlightened and achieve the highest consciousness possible, you need to understand that, deep down, court cards are all the same. Just like humans and slugs.

1. Place your court cards face down on a flat surface and swirl them around with the palm of your hand. Notice how they already look near identical.
2. Gather the cards and lay them face up in a 4 x 4 grid.
3. Starting with the top row, you must find something that all of those four court cards have in common. Try to be mature about this. Saying they all have faces might be temporarily amusing but you're only cheating yourself. Consider the whole card including clothing, accessories, companions and scenery. Try to be as specific as possible. You'll feel prouder to discover they all wear rings than if you settled on the fact they all wear crowns.
4. When you've found what the first four cards have in common, do the same for the second row, then the third row and the fourth. Don't move on until you're satisfied you've come up with something really impressive for each foursome. When you've finished all four rows, repeat the process for the columns, from left to right.
5. After you've completed all four rows and all four columns, sort the cards back into their proper ranks of Page, Knight, Queen and King, and then into Wands, Cups, Swords and Pentacles, just to show them they haven't all morphed into one single organism.

Casting Couch

6 of Cups

You call that acting?! The character was two-dimensional, your motivation was paper thin, and you didn't move a muscle through the whole thing. If I didn't know any better, I'd say you were made of card! What's that? You are? Well, to be honest, I've seen worse. You're hired!

1. First, decide which film you're casting for. It could be your favorite film, the film you last saw, or that awful 1980s comedy starring *wotsisname* that for some reason has always stuck in your head.
2. Jot down the names of all the main characters in the film and some of the minor ones as well if you like. Don't write down more than 16 characters though – you might find those extra roles difficult to fill. If you don't know a character's name just describe them, e.g., "the guy who turns up half-way through claiming to be her husband."
3. Make a note of each character's traits and physical attributes next to their name. This is what you're looking for in the auditions.
4. Place all the court cards face-up in front of you. Feel free to automatically cast any that are flirting with you – they've clearly got what it takes.
5. Now audition each of the remaining court cards. One by one, compare them to the notes you've made on the characters. How well do they fit in terms of age, appearance, attitude and screen presence? Don't worry about crossing gender boundaries. There's no reason why your male Knight of Cups can't play a female character. It worked for *Tootsie*.
6. If you're not sure whether a court is right for the role, imagine them saying lines from the movie. If you get goose bumps, you know you're on to a winner.
7. Be firm when it comes to rejections. Tell the actors in no uncertain terms why they didn't make the cut. It's okay to hurt their feelings – actors need to suffer for their art.
8. When you've finished casting all the roles, give your lead actors huge sums of money and send the unsuccessful ones back to their day jobs waiting tables.

Happy Families

7 of Cups

Families, eh? Can't live with them...yet you have to. But did you know that court cards also suffer from familial discord? It's a common misconception that members of court card families come from the same stock, like Mr. and Mrs. Pentacle and the two little Pentacles. In truth, most are unsuited, unbalanced, undignified, and understandably unhinged...

1. Shuffle the court cards together until they complain about the lack of personal space.
2. Turn the cards face up and look through them. Deal off the first Page, Knight, Queen and King you find that are each from different suits then put the rest of the cards to one side. The four people you behold are now members of the same family. You should already see the friction building.
3. Take a moment to decide everyone's role in the family and what relation they are to each other. Don't feel you need to stick to the nuclear family template of Mum, Dad, and the kids. Instead, be led by the cards themselves. If the King looks old, he might be an uncle, a grandfather, or even a great–grandfather. If he's young, maybe he's the big brother, or second cousin twice-removed who's come to stay for the summer *hols*.
4. Once everyone knows their place, look at how the family members get on. Imagine they live in the same house (or royal palace). Who runs the roost? Who causes the most trouble? Who picks up the pieces? Who's the black sheep?
5. Look too at individual relationships. How do the Page and the Knight get on? What about the Page and the Queen? How do they treat each other? What do they have in common? How do they get on each other's nerves? What do they say about the other person under their breath and what, deep down, do they secretly appreciate?
6. Once you've got a handle on the family dynamic, put it to the test. Send them on an all-expenses paid trip to a tiny cabin in the woods, with no TV, no internet, no phone and no possible form of escape. Remember, whatever doesn't kill them will only make them stronger.

How Do I Love Thee

8 of Cups

Roses are red, violets are blue,
I'm not a poet, that much is true.
But if you'll allow me, I'll make you a ditty,
Pass the thesaurus, you look very pretty –
And lovely and bonny and goodly and bright,
And stately and gracious, you're such a nice sight.
Your eyes flash with passion, your hair's golden fronds,
You look like a princess, you're my Queen of Pentacles...

1. Pick one court card at random. If you fancy a challenge, try the one you feel least attracted to.
2. Gaze at the court as though they are an angel descended from heaven. (If you happen to have one of those angel-themed decks, all the better.) Look at the court as if you're seeing them for the first time. Imagine they're the most beautiful creature you have ever seen. Let yourself be swept away by their loveliness. Continue to be swept away until you feel the urge to write a poem about them.
3. Now, jot down what you consider to be the four most wonderful things about the object of your affection – be it their noble countenance, their statuesque posture, their sparkling eyes or their stylish shoes. If you're struggling to find anything wonderful, just jot down the four things that you hate the least.
4. For each of those four things, write down a few adjectives that best describe their deliciousness. So, for example, you might decide the Knight of Swords' armor is hard, glistening, smooth, and well–oiled. Or you might think that the Queen of Pentacles has ripe, juicy, fleshy knees.
5. To have any hope of winning your heart's desire's heart, you must turn your list of random words into a lyrical masterpiece – a poem at once tender and passionate, one that will make them covet you instantly. You should spend at least four months crafting the perfect ode.
6. When you have finished your poem, read it to your beloved. Hopefully, by the time you reach the end, they will feel the same about you, but don't feel too bad if they don't. As the saying goes, there are plenty more courts in the deck...

Lonely Hearts

9 of Cups

Everybody needs somebody to love. Yes, even the Queen of Swords. Oh, she might seem romantically–challenged but who can say? Maybe beneath that icy cold exterior lurks a love of puppies and a yearning to take walks by the sea with that special someone. But will she ever find her soul mate? And who, exactly, is she looking for?

1. Place the Queen of Swords in front of you and put the rest of the court cards to one side.
2. Imagine she is going to place a lonely hearts ad in the newspaper – or whatever passes for a newspaper in the world of your deck.
3. First, consider how she might describe herself. Remember that she's going to want to make herself sound as appealing as possible so "scathing and insensitive" might not be the way to go. Be brief (as she's paying by the word) and try to include some physical description as well.
4. Now think about what she's seeking in a mate. What does she value? What does she enjoy? What does she need?
5. Once you've written the perfect lonely hearts ad, one that can't fail to attract Mr. Right (or King Right or Queen Right), bring back the other court cards. Let the Queen of Swords get a good look at each and every one. Which one is her perfect match?
6. If the answer is "no one," don't despair. Go through the rest of the deck, card by card, desperately seeking a soul mate. Let not status be an obstacle to love. If the person who will make the Queen of Swords happy turns out to be a pauper, a peasant or a pixie, so be it.
7. Toast the happy couple with a glass of champagne – but don't think your work is done. When the other courts get a whiff of your matchmaking skills, they'll be knocking down your door to find them love.

Tall, Dark Stranger

10 of Cups

I see a great love in your future. He has black hair and dark eyes. He's tall and handsome. Wait! There's more... He's wearing blue jeans and a red T-shirt with the words "Pete's Eels" printed on the back. He walks with a pronounced limp. He has a scar over his right eye and a tattoo of a fish playing football on his left shoulder. Whaddya mean "No"?

1. For this to be effective, you must isolate yourself. Retreat to a room without windows, or to a secret hideaway where you won't be disturbed. You must not be able to see another human being (cats are allowed, though).
2. Hopefully, you remembered to bring your court cards with you. If not, go and get them. Give them a cursory shuffle then spread them face-down before you in four rows of four.
3. Pick a card from the top row and turn it face up. This card tells you about the next person you'll lay eyes on. Study it to find out what they will look like. Make notes on the basics – hair color, eye color, age, height and build.
4. Now, choose a card from the second row for more details about the mystery person's physical appearance. Jot down how their hair is styled. Are they wearing make-up? What clothes or jewelry are they wearing? Even if the card doesn't depict an actual person, try to get an impression from the colors and shapes contained in the image.
5. Pick a card in the third row to get clues about how the mystery person walks and talks. Are their movements quick and precise or slow and lumbering? What do they do with their hands when they're speaking? What's their posture like? How would they sit in a chair?
6. Finally, choose a card from the bottom row and examine it very closely. Use details from this card to add specifics to the description. Will the next person you meet have any distinguishing features, such as moles or scars? Will they have any tattoos or piercings? Is there anything else noticeable about them – for example, do they have wings? Add as much detail as you can.

7. Now turn all the cards face down again and review your notes. Build a picture in your mind's eye of the person your cards say you're going to meet. Then gather up your cards, leave your solitary confinement and rejoin society. Try not to pass out from shock as you immediately run into a seven-foot-tall, white-haired Elf King wearing a winged helmet and a pink cloak.

In Therapy

Page of Cups

Many Tarotists agree that the court cards are extremely challenging. That's because, like a human, each court is a highly complex individual who carries around a lot of deep-seated anxiety and a whole suitcase full of emotional baggage. Here's how you can get to know the neurotic, dysfunctional, obsessive-compulsive, passive-aggressive, scaredy cat hidden inside...

1. There's no time to waste. All court cards are as screwed up as the next guy, so you've got your work cut out. Pick a card at random and begin therapy straight away.
2. Lay the card on a couch and sit opposite, preferably in a reclining chair. Set a timer for one hour – that should give you long enough to fully examine all the court's demons, inhibitions and hang-ups.
3. Allow an awkward silence to settle over the room. If you have a clock with a loud tick, use it to full effect. Tap your pen thoughtfully on your notepad as you study your patient. When they look like they're about to crack, ask them one probing question from the list that follows.

4. Now listen very carefully. Allow the court to speak in their own time, using their own words. Many patients in therapy are nervous at first, but as a trained professional, you should be able to pick up a lot from body language alone. You know what they want to say, even if they can't say it. Make notes and nod sympathetically as they expose their soul. Offer a tissue if one is needed.

5. When you're satisfied you've explored that subject fully, move on with another question. Try to cover as much ground as possible in the time you have but don't push the court too hard. If necessary, schedule a second appointment – you can bill double.

6. When the hour is up, thank your patient for opening up to you. Reassure them that everyone has problems and it will all be okay. Make a nice cup of tea and share a packet of biscuits with them until they feel strong enough to face the world again.

7. Remember, everything you've learned in the past hour must be kept strictly confidential. Consider filing your notes in a locked cabinet or, better yet, bury them in the garden and cover them with a thicket of brambles.

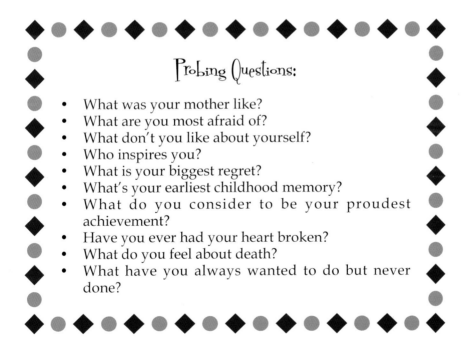

Probing Questions:

- What was your mother like?
- What are you most afraid of?
- What don't you like about yourself?
- Who inspires you?
- What is your biggest regret?
- What's your earliest childhood memory?
- What do you consider to be your proudest achievement?
- Have you ever had your heart broken?
- What do you feel about death?
- What have you always wanted to do but never done?

Strike Up the Band

Knight of Cups

Have you noticed how some of the court cards suffer from bigheadedness? You know the ones – always jostling for the limelight, always striking a pose, always trying to get noticed. These are the wannabe celebrities in the deck. They have to make an entrance any time they turn up in a reading. All that's missing is the rapturous applause and signature theme tune...

1. Spread all the court cards out before you and pick the one that's crying "Me, Me, Me" the loudest. Relegate the rest to the sidelines.
2. Stand the spotlight-seeking court in front of you. Shine a spotlight on them. Notice how pleased they are at getting their own way.
3. Now, size them up. Make them move around and strut their stuff. What kind of person are they? What do they most want people to notice about them? What signature tune would they choose for themselves if they could? What music would they want to be playing every time they entered a room?
4. Next, shake 'em down. Hone in on their flaws – the weaknesses they're hoping you don't notice. What music would suit the real person behind the celebrity mask?
5. Decide if you want to let them keep their grandiose affectations. If so, let them have the music they want. Let it play every time they turn up in a spread. Otherwise, well, maybe repeatedly hearing the other tune you chose for them will deflate their insufferable ego.

Off With Their Heads!

Queen of Cups

Court cards are so together aren't they? They never question who they are, they never feel confused or contradicted. You never see court cards going off on some spiritual journey to "find themselves." Imagine a court card having an identity crisis. The very idea...

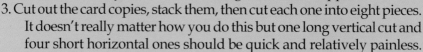

1. Make color copies of all 16 court cards, using a photocopier, a scanner, or an artist friend who's not above knocking up some forgeries. Make them the same size or larger than the originals.

2. Return the real court cards to the deck and place them far, far away from the operating table. Preferably in another building. Accidents happen.

3. Cut out the card copies, stack them, then cut each one into eight pieces. It doesn't really matter how you do this but one long vertical cut and four short horizontal ones should be quick and relatively painless.

4. Put all the pieces into a bag or lidded container and shake until they're well mixed up (both physically and psychologically). Pour them out onto a large flat surface.

5. Now, if you're mature and you respect your court cards, you'll attempt to piece them all back together in the quickest time possible. If, however, you're feeling wicked, you might like to see what kind of new courts you can make, using different bits of each card.

6. Remember: Never EVER chop up your actual Tarot cards. It doesn't matter how skilled you are at piecing them back together, the psychological damage you'll inflict will scar them for life.

Mia Familiar

King of Cups

Having a pet can be a great source of comfort and joy, so what better way is there to show your court cards you care than to give each of them a hand-picked companion? Whether it's a gecko or a goose, a horse or a hippopotamus, your gift will provide each court with friendship, unconditional love, and cuddles – unless it's a crocodile, of course...

1. Select the loneliest-looking court card from your deck.
2. Study the court to decide what creature would give them the most pleasure. You can choose anything you like, be it animal, bird, reptile, insect, or fish. You could even choose a fantastical creature such as a dragon, a unicorn, or a labradoodle. Try to find a creature that complements the court's appearance, style or temperament.
3. Once you've found the perfect pet, find or draw a picture of it and cut it out so your court can spend time with it. If they want to, let the court name their new companion. You could even make a special petting zoo to keep near your deck which your courts can visit whenever they feel sad or stressed.

Hot Gossip

Ace of Swords

Scandal, intrigue, blackmail, seduction – it's just another ordinary day in Tarot's royal courts. And who can blame them? It's so boring sitting around on thrones and no one can be bothered to go to war. A little gossip here and there, perhaps a touch of backstabbing, helps to break the monotony. Really, what harm can it do?

1. Shuffle the court cards until they're buzzing with hearsay and rumor, then place any five of them face up in a row. Set the rest aside within eavesdropping distance.
2. Study the cards to find out what they're hiding. Body language can be especially revealing. Move the cards around if necessary – this will make them uneasy and more likely to give something away. Answer ALL of the following questions and remember, don't let a little thing like truth stand in the way of a good story.

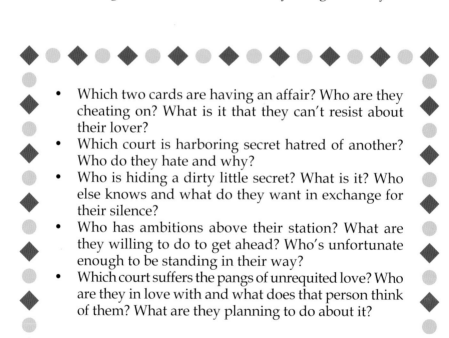

- Which two cards are having an affair? Who are they cheating on? What is it that they can't resist about their lover?
- Which court is harboring secret hatred of another? Who do they hate and why?
- Who is hiding a dirty little secret? What is it? Who else knows and what do they want in exchange for their silence?
- Who has ambitions above their station? What are they willing to do to get ahead? Who's unfortunate enough to be standing in their way?
- Which court suffers the pangs of unrequited love? Who are they in love with and what does that person think of them? What are they planning to do about it?

3. Don't stop there. The wonderful thing about rumors is their ability to snowball. What would happen if you added another court or two to the mix? Imagine their tiny ripples making waves for the others.
4. Finally, pick one of the cards and take them aside. Ask them to dish the dirt on the other courts. What would they say about them behind their backs?
5. When you've recovered from the shock, shuffle all the courts back together and leave them to their business. You can always come back tomorrow if you can't bear to miss out on the latest gossip.

The Dark Side

2 of Swords

It's the 21st Century. Cities are cleaner. Computers are smaller. Robots do what we tell them to (for now). Yet the ancient battle between good and evil rages on. Somewhere, deep inside a Tarot deck, darkness has gained a small victory. Somewhere, someone has turned to the dark side. Evil, thy name is…the Page of Cups?

1. Lay all the court cards in front of you and pick the one that looks the most malevolent. If malevolent is too strong a word, try "sinister," "scheming," or "a little bit moody," until you've singled out the court card most likely to stray from the path of righteousness.
2. Put the other courts back in your good books and focus on the bad boy or girl in front of you.
3. Imagine this court's journey into the heart of darkness has already begun. Behind those noble eyes, world domination plans are already being hatched. Study the card for clues as to what those fiendish plans might be. Small, innocent details (cats, especially) can hide the most dastardly of plots. Try not to be tricked by a charming smile. Pay close attention instead to what their hands are doing.
4. Imagine this court is the most evil person in the world. Or, if not the most evil person in the world, the most evil person in a movie adaptation of a comic book. Drawing from what you can see in the card, how would they act? How would they talk? What would their underground-or-otherwise lair look like? In everyday conversation, would they refer to themselves in the third person? Would they act alone or would they gather an army of revenge-seeking cats?
5. Finally, to make the court's transformation complete, give them a name. Make it a good one…or rather, make it a really *evil* one. If you shiver every time you think of it, all the better. If you must speak it aloud, use a hushed whisper.
6. Now, reverse the process. Obviously you can't allow an evil genius to take up residence in your Tarot deck so you must return the

court card to their normal, do–gooding self. Banish the darkness by reminding them of their favorite things. Surround them with their friends and loved ones. Bathe them in warm sunshine. Fluffy bunnies, fairy dust, and rainbows are all useful allies in the battle against eternal darkness.

7. If things go well, consider allowing all the other courts to confront their inner Baddie. For it is only by coming face to face with their dark sides that they can truly call themselves enlightened.

King For a Day

3 of Swords

Making decisions is hard. First you have to weigh up the pros and cons, then you have to consider the internal and external factors, then you have to think about the consequences. And that's just to work out what coffee you want. Wouldn't it be easier if someone else made all your decisions for you?

1. Place your cards next to your bed before you go to sleep and do this activity as soon as you wake up in the morning.
2. Shuffle the court cards; then rap them on the table three times to summon your best advisor.
3. Turn over the top card and place it in front of you. Send the rest away to breathe a sigh of relief.
4. The card you've chosen has actually been chosen for you to be your advisor for the day. So you can immediately stop worrying about whether you've made the right decision. Thus begins your foray into the wonderful world of zero culpability.
5. Throughout the day, whenever a decision is required of you, you must defer to your royal court advisor. Whatever choice arises, whatever question hovers over your head, you must summon your advisor, explain your dilemma and ask them what you should do. Then you must listen and do what they say.
6. If at any time you feel your advisor doesn't have your best interests at heart, fire them. It may be that they are attempting to undermine your authority in order to stage a coup.

115

Behind Closed Doors

4 of Swords

So you think you know each court? Well, think again. So far they've only let you see what they want you to see. If you want true intimacy, you need to see them at their most vulnerable, and you need to enter into their most private, sacred space. But beware – once you've seen the King of Pentacles in a romper suit, it's almost impossible to erase it from your memory...

1. Do this late at night, when your cards are sleepy.
2. Choose a court card and place them on a table in front of you. Sit on a comfortable, supportive chair with your feet flat on the floor and spaced shoulder-width apart. Rest your hands on the table either side of the card.
3. Gaze calmly at the court. Breathe in through your nose and out through your mouth. Let your eyelids droop a little until your vision softens.
4. When you feel ready, ask the court for permission to enter the room where they sleep. If they allow you, close your eyes and imagine them showing you the way. If they are not willing, abandon the exercise. They'll let you know when they're ready.
5. Follow the court where they take you. Imagine them opening the door to their private quarters. Step inside quietly and stand discreetly next to a wall so as not to disturb them. Watch them as they get ready for bed. Pay attention to their little rituals, the things they do to make themselves feel comfortable and safe. Pay attention to what they surround themselves with. Pay attention to the most important thing of all – their bed. Watch them get in and settle down to sleep.
6. When they're fast asleep and their breathing is quiet and steady, tiptoe out of the room and carefully close the door. Watch out for the creaky floorboard!
7. Now open your eyes. Thank the court for sharing with you and kiss them good night. Then go to bed and sleep deeply, blissfully unaware that all the court cards are in your room spying on you.

Part Four

Just My Archetype

22 Ways to Make It With the Majors

A Town Called Tarot

5 of Swords

Welcome to Tarot (pop. 22) – a small town with big ideas. A place where Fools walk the streets, where Lovers meet, where Hermits retreat. A place where you can hang with the Man, play chicken run with the Chariot and dance with the Devil. A place limited only by your imagination and the size of your paper...

1. You will need a large sheet of white paper. If you don't have one, tape 6–8 sheets of standard size paper together or commandeer a bed sheet. (It's okay; it's for important Tarot business.)
2. Shuffle the Major Arcana. Place all the cards face down in random positions on the sheet of paper.
3. Turn one card face up and imagine it represents a person or place in a fictional town. If it's a person, who? Where do they live or what job do they do? What is their name? If you feel the card represents a place, what is it called, and what function does it serve in the town? Small towns always have their fair share of eccentrics so give your imagination free rein.
4. As you imagine each card coming to life, draw a bird's eye view of your vision on the paper. Sketch people and buildings and connect them by roads and paths. Label each drawing to show what it is. Add to the environment with parks, rivers, beaches and mountain ranges. Spend time adding small details specific to your cards to make your town seem more real.
5. If you're enjoying this, go even deeper by dreaming up background stories for your townsfolk. Let them go about their business and show you what their world is like. Keep the map of your town handy and bring it out on rainy days. Play on it using your Major Arcana cards like dolls. Ignore the concerned whisperings of your family and friends. You don't need them – the people of Tarot Town are your friends now…

Between the Lines

6 of Swords

Did you know bibliomancy is the art of interpreting random passages from the Bible and other sacred texts, whereas stichomancy is the term given to divination using any old book you find lying around? Of course, there's also comicomancy, manualomancy and glossomancy (divination using women's magazines) – any of which are suitable for this exercise...

1. You will need a large selection of books. If your house does not have its own library, use the public library instead.
2. Shuffle the Major Arcana cards; then hold them as you walk along the bookshelves. You should feel a pull towards one of the shelves. Move your hands across the spines of the books until your cards glow, or a book jumps off the shelf, or until you get that special feeling about one book in particular.
3. Set your cards down and balance the book on its spine in your left hand. Close your eyes and allow the book to open where it will. Use the index finger of your right hand to randomly select a paragraph from either of the two revealed pages.
4. Open your eyes and read the passage your unconscious mind has chosen. Then, turn over the top card of your deck.
5. Think about what you have read and what the card is showing you. You should aim to find some common thread between them, which you can then weave into a rich and deeply satisfying insight. Work out how the text complements the image and how the image illuminates the text.
6. When you have finished, return the book to its original place on the shelf and – if you are in a public library – leave quickly before anyone starts asking questions.

The House That Tarot Built

7 of Swords

A pair of elegant Greco-Roman columns channel us into a private back room where rich drapes hang from ceiling to floor, festooned in a glorious pomegranate motif. The walls are painted sky blue and everywhere you look there are references to the crescent moon. Who would live in a house like this? The High Priestess? Actually, no...

1. Choose one of the rooms in your house. It could be the room you feel most relaxed in, the room where you spend most time with family, or the room you last sneezed in. Go to that room now and kneel on the floor facing north.
2. Shuffle your Major Arcana cards and select one at random. Lay it face up in front of you and put the rest of the cards to one side.
3. Take a moment to soak up the ambience of the card. Allow your eyes to follow every line and let them sink deeply into the colors. Is the card harmonious or full of contrast? Is it soothing or vibrant? Take note of any recurring shapes. Retrieve your eyes before proceeding.
4. Now turn your attention to the room. Imagine decorating it in the style of this card. What color would you paint the walls? What kind of furniture would you buy? What fabric could you use for the drapes? Also consider accents such as cushions, rugs, art, vases, sculpture and lighting. Try to capture the mood of the card in your imaginary decor.
5. When you've finished, think about whether the card you selected actually suits the room you're in. How does it make you feel? If you like what you see in your mind's eye, maybe you should try the makeover for real. Imagine every room decorated in the style of a different card: "Let's eat in the Hierophantery tonight, darling."

A You're Adorable

8 of Swords

Major Arcana cards have it all: looks, brains, power, massive egos. They know as well as anyone (better than anyone) how important they are. Yet without we humans constantly singing their praises, they would surely succumb to low self esteem and crumble into the ether. Or maybe not. Either way, it's a good idea to keep morale up...

1. Select one of the Major Arcana cards at random or choose the card that seems most in need of a pick-me-up. Stand it in a prominent position – perhaps propping it against a tin of beans.
2. On a sheet of paper, list all 26 letters of the alphabet (or, if you're reading this in Hebrew, all 22). Then, with great care and serious contemplation, find a single perfect word starting with each of the letters (hyphens allowed) which describes the card or some aspect of it.
3. Don't feel you only have to list nice things. If you think a card is arrogant, bloody-minded, or cold, say so! You may feel you're being cruel, but if you can't be honest, how will your card ever have the opportunity to change?
4. When you have finished (without cheating, yes you have to do "q" and "x"), read your list of words so the card can hear them. If it isn't immediately clear why you have chosen certain words ("quilty" and "xanthous" for example) take a moment to explain what you mean.
5. Finish the session with a group hug then return the card to the pack so it can crow over its peers with renewed narcissistic vigor.

Everything Counts

9 of Swords

Difficulty sleeping? Counting sheep just not working for you? You're not alone. Did you know counting sheep has been clinically proven to be only "somewhat" effective for inducing sleep? Why not try counting Tarot? It's more grueling than watching farmyard animals jump fences and way more fun! Yours for only $99.95 (doesn't include shipping or taxes, sleep effect not guaranteed).

1. Turn off the lights and snuggle in bed with the Major Arcana cards, a torch, and a mug of warm milk.
2. Hold your cards under the duvet and pick one at random. Tuck all the other cards under your pillow.
3. Using the torch, study your chosen card closely. Find something in the image that there is only one of. Next, find something that there is only two of. Then find something there is only three of. Then find something there is only four of. You get the idea.
4. It's likely you'll get stuck at some point. If so, just skip that number and move onto the next. No one will ever know.
5. Keep going until you fall asleep or run out of things to count (in which case you'll need to resort to counting sheep again).

Dancing With the Devil

10 of Swords

Have you ever seen a Fool foxtrot? What about a Magician doing the mashed potato? The Tower can really twist, don't you know, and there ain't nobody can do the funky chicken like the Chariot. Oh yes, the Major Arcana can really bust a move. Dancing with the Stars? You ain't seen nothin' yet...

1. Hold the Major Arcana cards in both hands then close your eyes and throw all the cards into the air. NEVER do this outside during high winds. The card that lands closest to your left foot will be your partner for this dance. Move the rest of the cards away from the dance floor so they can ~~mock your technique~~ watch you with admiration and envy.
2. Select a piece of music that you would like to dance to. Don't heed your partner's requests – if you let them have their way, the Emperor wouldn't listen to anything but marching songs and Death would only choose dirges. Put on whatever suits your mood, whether that's Beethoven, Black Sabbath, or the Birdie Song.
3. As soon as the music starts, grab your partner and dance. Hold the card whichever way feels right. The important thing is that you both dance together so don't get all shy and leave them standing in the middle of the dance floor. Dance until the music stops, until one or both of you collapse with exhaustion, or until you're voted off by the public.

Rude Rhymes

Page of Swords

Acquaintances exchange polite compliments. Buddies avoid mentioning each other's faults. But true friends – true friends love poking fun. Be a good friend to your Tarot cards today...

1. Swirl the Major Arcana cards face down in front of you then choose one at random and turn it face up.
2. Imagine you're one of those super-talented caricaturists, trying to pay your way by drawing people on a busy street. You've just finished a scathingly accurate portrait of an ex-Army major and are looking for your next victim. Who should walk by but one of the Tarot archetypes...
3. Study the trump in front of you with a satirist's sharp eye (ask the satirist for permission first) and decide which of its features is most ripe for ridicule. Now, grab a pen and start limericking! If you're not too sure what to write, use the examples below to help you. It's easier if you begin with the second line and then tailor the first line to rhyme with it. Make sure you base your limerick entirely on what you see in front of you and remember – lampooning your Tarot cards is a simple way to show them how much you care, so be as cheeky as you like. They won't mind a bit...
4. Make sure line one rhymes with lines two and five, and that lines three and four rhyme with each other. Got it?
5. When you've finished, memorize the limerick and use it to lighten the mood when you're up to your solar plexus in a serious reading.

There once was a Hermit with woes,
Cause his beard grew right down to his toes.
When asked, "Do you step on it?"
He replied, "You can bet on it –
That's why I've broken my nose."

There was a young Emperor called Ted,
Who ruled without wearing a thread.
He thought it was cool
Though he looked like a Fool,
But he still wore his crown on his head.

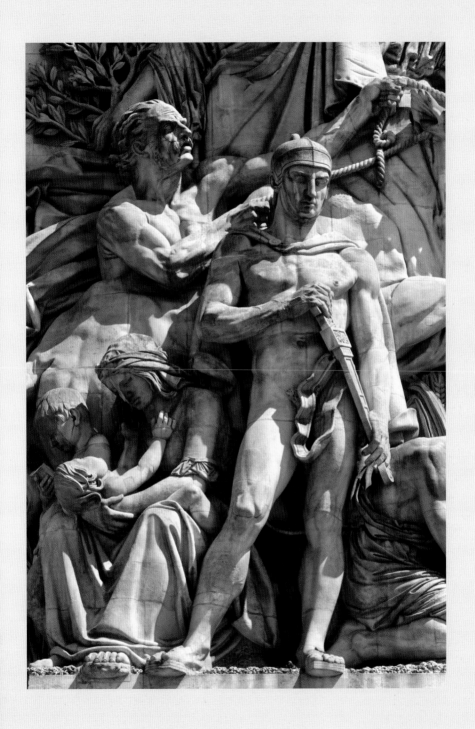

Skin Deep

Knight of Swords

If there's one thing Tarot teaches us, it's to look beyond the surface, to see the barely visible patterns hidden within all that exists; to look for meaning where most would see none; to reach deep into our own souls and the souls of those we meet to discover the parts we all play in the great mystery of life. But more than that, it's that Tarot cards are just so darn pretty...

1. Spread the Major Arcana cards out before you, allowing each one enough space to shine its unique light.
2. Based on appearances alone, pick the card you find least attractive and place it to the very left of the cards. Don't worry, it's just a bit of cardboard, it can't take it personally. Probably.
3. Arrange the remaining cards to the right of this card. Think carefully and place them in order of attractiveness. You should finish up with the cards assembled in a glorious sliding scale of loveliness, ranging from "meh" to "so gorgeous I want to eat it." Sigh contentedly as you gaze upon them.
4. When you've finished and the very prettiest card is seated to the right of all the other cards, award it a shiny crown, a purple sash, and an enormous bouquet of flowers. Applaud appreciatively as it takes a bow.

Outside the Box

Queen of Swords

Tarot cards: they're so... small, aren't they? All that wisdom, accumulated over centuries of humankind's questing for spiritual knowledge, represented by pretty pictures of peasants waving sticks about – all crammed into a rectangle no bigger than a hand. Can you imagine what would happen if your Tarot cards could break through their borders? Don't worry, they can't...

1. Select one Major Arcana card, either deliberately or at random and put the others aside. If they complain, tell them they'll all get a turn and they should spend the time discussing big philosophical questions or what to have for dinner.
2. Place the card you chose face-up in the middle of a sheet of paper.
3. Draw a light, barely discernable line around the card; then move the card off the paper.
4. As accurately as you can, copy the image of the card inside the outline you've drawn but instead of stopping at the outline, continue your drawing right up to the edges of the paper. Try to depict what lies outside the confines of the card. Extend the landscape and background scenery and add in other people. Place the card in a larger context.
5. Don't think too hard about what to draw. Imagine you're a three year old let loose with the crayons (but try not to draw on any walls).
6. When you've finished drawing, stand back to admire your work. Marvel at the amazing discoveries you've made about the world your card inhabits. Wonder at the brilliance of your intuitive insights. Quick, run and show someone!
7. Keep your picture stuck on the fridge door as a metaphor for the incredible ability of the human soul to constantly search for understanding beyond the limits of the known physical universe. And to show off your drawing skills.

Wisdom of the Majors

King of Swords

If you need advice, ask your best friend. If your best friend's out of town, ask your mum. If your mum just doesn't get it, ask grandma. If grandma's too busy street dancing, there's only one place left to turn. Not only are the Major Arcana cards wise and profound; they also have aeons of time on their hands and are only too happy to spend it enlightening you...

1. First, think of a problem for which you could use some advice. If your life is currently problem-free, consider seeing a therapist to help you dredge up some hidden trauma.
2. Shuffle the Major Arcana whilst inwardly stewing about your problem.
3. Kneel or sit on the floor and deal the Major Arcana cards face-down in a rough semi-circle in front of you.
4. Close your eyes and ask the cards to grace you with their infinite wisdom.
5. Start with the card nearest your left hand. Turn it face up. Stop, look, and listen. Wait for the card to speak. Do not feel tempted to hurry it up. It takes time to be profound.
6. When receiving the wisdom of the Tarot elders in this way, don't be disappointed with what may appear to be trivial statements. The Major Arcana cards may be powerful but they still have to communicate using our simple human language and thus, great insight may be disguised within simple phrases. For example, the Empress says "The daffodils are lovely at this time of year, don't you think? Always such happy faces." Write it down so you can ponder its great wisdom over time.
7. Once the card has spoken, turn it face down again to prevent it from waffling on. Do the same for all 22 cards then review your notes. Take whatever wisdom is most beneficial and ignore the rest.

The Devil's in the Details

Ace of Pentacles

Interpreting Tarot cards is like trying to solve a mysterious puzzle. All the pieces are there, you just have to work out how they fit together. Good decks make it easy by using recurring motifs – all you have to do is spot them. Could it be those trees? The color yellow? The Knight's disdainful expression and the Emperor's scowl? Wait! Who put that grandfather clock there?

1. Shuffle the Major Arcana cards in with the rest of the deck. Do this vigorously and carelessly until you suspect one or more of the trumps have accidentally acquired items that don't belong to them.
2. Cut the pack in the middle and look through the bottom half until you come to a Major Arcana card. Place it in front of you and put the rest aside.
3. Study the card, preferably using one of those tiny magnifying glasses that jewelers use to appraise diamonds. Start at the top left corner and move across the card in broad, slow strokes. Examine the whole card this way before proceeding to the next step.
4. Now repeat step 3, but this time pretend you are a world-famous and made-for-TV detective, whose inquisitive mind and eagle eyes never fail to spot the slightest incongruity. Painstakingly scour the card for some small detail that sticks out. Possibly, it is something that clearly doesn't belong – a bicycle in an Arthurian court, perhaps; more likely, it will be something far more subtle: a bubble on a leaf, or an arrow lying at the Empress's feet.
5. Now, the fun begins! Using only your keen intuitive senses and your innate powers of making stuff up, you must work out how and why that object came to be there. Every *Thing* has a story. Where did it come from? How did it arrive in this place, at this time? Who put it there? What would it tell you if it could speak?
6. It may help to work backwards, piecing the story together bit by bit by asking yourself questions. For example: How did the arrow get on the floor? It flew through the window. Why did it fly through the window? It was shot by a knight who was startled by a stag, causing the arrow to fly off in the wrong direction. What was he aiming for? He was trying to sever the rope that tied his beloved horse to the

Empress's gatepost. Why was his horse tied to the post? Because the Empress took a fancy to it, after hearing that it could count to 20 on one hoof.

7. And so on…

8. Once you're satisfied you've explained the presence of the aforementioned object, your work here is done. Now, whenever you see this card, you can recall the story and use it to cast a richer, deeper, more confusing light on your readings.

Instant Expert

2 of Pentacles

If you want to be an expert on your deck, you need to behave as if you know more about it than anyone else. There are three ways to do this:

A. Spend ten years on a mountaintop with only your cards and a yak for company.

B. Track down the creator of the deck and pester them with questions about the hidden meaning of every card.

C. Talk about the cards in such a way that people will assume the deck itself chose you to share its message with the world.

Obviously, A and B aren't serious suggestions...

1. For the purposes of this exercise, select one Major Arcana card at random, with your eyes closed, using only your nose. If, however, you are amongst other Tarotists, sharing Tarot anecdotes or exchanging readings, you can carry out the following sequence using any card under discussion. Be prepared for some pretty strong reactions from your peers, which will range from barely disguised jealousy to outright disgust at your obvious superiority.
2. Place the chosen card before you. Close your mouth and breathe in deeply, savoring the card's distinctive bouquet. Waft your hands in front of your face to aid the passage of scent up your nostrils.
3. Hold the card up to the light to appreciate its clarity and color. Turn it around and try to see through the back.
4. Stick your tongue out and gently lick the face of the card. Take a moment to fully comprehend the body and flavor of the card.
5. Now, if you are alone, make notes. You have just experienced the card in a way that very few people ever have. You have a responsibility to share what you've learned with the world, so that those who dare not venture so far in search of wisdom may benefit from your courage and vision. Imagine the card is a fine

wine and describe it accordingly: "The Hermit is an enigmatic blend of black cherry and musk, shrouded in an inky, syrupy concoction that can only be described as liquid anti–matter." If in company, immediately pronounce your findings, then quickly replace the card and walk away to preclude any further discussion on the matter.

6. Collate your opinions on each card into a short pamphlet which you can then self-publish and distribute via local bus stations and park benches.

Face Off

3 of Pentacles

In this age of equality, it might seem wrong to talk about which Major Arcana is better than all the others. But a little competition never hurt anyone and Tarot cards, like wolves, are happiest when they know their place in the pack. Stage this tournament to reveal which card is the Alpha Major and who will be crowned the top trump...

1. Shuffle the Major Arcana cards until they're fired up and ready to rumble.
2. Deal them face down in two horizontal rows of 11 cards each, one directly below the other.
3. The cards are going to duel so start with the pair of cards in the left-most column. For each pair of cards, pick any attribute from the Attributes list that follows, then turn both cards face up. It's up to you to decide which card trumps the other in terms of that attribute. Place the winner in a separate pile above the two rows and discard the loser.
4. In the case of a draw (you can't decide or it's just too close to call) turn both cards face down, shuffle them in with any remaining face-down cards and deal them out again.
5. When all 11 duels are over you'll be left with a pile of 11 winners. Shuffle this pile and remove one card to start a new winners pile – this is the "wild card" and it gets a free pass to the next round because of the odd number. Pair up the remaining cards as you did before for a new round of duels. Repeat this process until one mighty major emerges triumphant.

Attributes

Biggest	Which card depicts the biggest person, building, animal or thing?
Fastest	Which card looks like it would beat the other in a race?
Most Powerful	Which card most makes your knees tremble?
Most Clever	Which card is most intelligent and better at chess?
Most Attractive	Which card turns the most heads?

The Old School Tie

4 of Pentacles

Ah, school days. Remember trying to stay awake in history lessons? Shuffling awkwardly in the corner at the prom? *Literally* dying of embarrassment because you got a spot on the first day back after summer break? Of course you don't. You've blocked it all from memory thanks to years of therapy. Well, here's something that should make it all come flooding back...

1. Shuffle the Major Arcana and single out one card. Make it stand at the front of the class.
2. Take a pencil and some scrap paper and, using the card as inspiration, draw a school emblem, such as would be found on a blazer or on the front of the report card you "lost." You should aim to keep your design simple but incorporate the important visual elements of the card.
3. Color the emblem in using your old school colors. If that's too traumatic, just pick two or three colors that look nice together.
4. Consider your emblem and sum up the values that it represents. Beneath it, write a motto based on the qualities of the card. For example, some typical school mottos include: "I Will Endure," "Integrity, Valor, High Grades," and "Seen and Not Heard." For added gravitas, translate your motto into Latin.
5. Spend the rest of the day trying to live according to your new motto. It may help to cut out your emblem and pin it to your chest where everyone can see it.

Religious Zeal

5 of Pentacles

When you feel lost, Tarot is there. When you get cross, Tarot is there. When you can't find your socks, Tarot is there. Isn't it about time Tarot got some thanks?

1. You are going to bring forth a Tarot god or goddess (henceforth known as the God/dess). Unfortunately, Tarot deities don't just come when they're called, so you must wait until the sun is at its zenith, all the planets are aligned, and the moon is blue before you attempt a summoning.
2. When the conditions are right, stand facing north and shuffle the Major Arcana. Kneel facing west then shuffle again. Turn to the south and shuffle a bit more, this time with your forehead touching the ground (this becomes easier with practice), then lie pointing eastwards for a final shuffle.
3. Place the cards face down in a neat pile in direct sunlight.
4. Rise to your feet without using your elbows, and walk clockwise around the cards three times. The card depicting the true God/dess of Tarot should now rise to the top of the pile, though it may be weak so you'll have to turn it over yourself. Do not gaze directly at it, but observe it out of the corner of your eyes.
5. You now have a duty to spread word of the new God/dess to the world. You are the chosen one – the prophet, the mouthpiece of the heavens. You are also the only person who knows of the God/dess's existence, which puts you in a very interesting position. It falls to you to decide how the God/dess should be worshipped and what particular rituals, quirks, and sacrifices will be required of its followers – and how they should dress.
6. Consider also the issue of commandments. Some gods like them, some don't. If yours does, be sure to write them down, preferably in stone. There's nothing worse than having to ask a supreme being to repeat themselves.
7. Finally, select one day of the year to be a special day for honoring the new God/dess. Mark it on your calendar and plan how you're going to celebrate. Set up a website so others can join in. Don't forget to make the God/dess the guest of honor.

Personal Effects

6 of Pentacles

The things we carry say a lot about us. For example, some nineteenth-century Arctic explorers thought it was very important to carry gramophones, silver tea services, and chess sets in their backpacks. Think about that for a moment. Fortunately, the Major Arcana have much more sense when it comes to lugging around unnecessary baggage. Or do they...?

1. You are going to take an inventory of *everything* on every Major Arcana card. For this you will need:

   • A ledger book, with lines so narrow you need a magnifying glass to write on them.
   • A magnifying glass.
   • A fine and distinguished pen, such as a fountain pen or a quill.

2. As you will be cataloguing every card, it is sensible to start at the beginning, with the Fool. Unless you believe that the Fool doesn't belong at the beginning, in which case start at the end.
3. Study the Fool very carefully. On the first page of your ledger, underneath the Fool's name, write down every item, symbol or UFO (Unidentified Foolish Object) that is on the card. Take great care to record the details of each item accurately, so instead of writing "a dog" write "one small terrier, white with one black ear, leaping."
4. When you are confident that you have documented everything that can been seen, take it one step further and add to the list everything that can't be seen. As the Chief Surveyor and *Inventorer* of Tarot (or CSI: Tarot), you would be remiss if you didn't look beyond the obvious. So also note what is in the Fool's bag, what the Magician has got up his sleeve, what the High Priestess is hiding behind her veil, etc.
5. Once every card has been inventoried, your ledger will prove invaluable in situations where you need to quickly check the color of Justice's petticoats or look up how many spokes there are on the Chariot's wheels. It will also prove priceless should your deck

ever become lost or stolen, as you can instantly provide a full description to the police so they can dedicate all their resources to retrieving it.

A Novel Approach

7 of Pentacles

They say everyone has at least one novel in them (hopefully not *War and Peace* or you'd get indigestion). But writing a novel is long, hard work which demands a lot of deep thought and repeated spell-checking. Wouldn't it be easier to just write the synopsis? That way, everyone can marvel at your thrilling plot and you can get on with something less stressful, like swimming with sharks…

1. Shuffle the Major Arcana cards then cut them into three piles.
2. Shuffle each pile individually then place them face down in a row.
3. Turn over the top card of the left-most pile. This card illustrates the beginning of your novel. You will immediately notice that it weaves the story on different levels. This card will give you:

- The setting for your novel
- The main character(s)
- The major event that propels your characters into action
- It will also suggest, of course, the grand theme or great idea – something like Love or Death or Taxes – that all events in the novel address in some way.

Take a moment to jot down all the sparks of inspiration that are flying around the room

4. Now turn over the top card of the middle pile. Here you should find:

- At least one other character (an enemy or an ally)
- Another event that complicates matters
- A second setting to keep things moving
- A crisis of epic proportions which throws everything and everyone into turmoil

Again, write as much or as little as you need to make sure you don't forget these dramatic turns of events.

5. Last, turn over the top card of the right-hand pile. In this, your novel's stunning denouement, all the threads of your plot will be wrapped up and tied in a neat little bow. Here you should look for:

- A solution to all your (plotting) problems
- An over-arching message or moral that illustrates what the characters have learned
- Another setting
- Some kind of climactic scene that would keep your readers reading to the very last page (if you ever got round to writing it)

6. Think you're finished? Think again. So far all you've got is a sequence of events. If you want to be a proper pretend novelist, you have to pull it all together by writing a synopsis – the kind of thrilling blurb that might grace the back cover of your nonexistent book. Start by focusing on your characters, drop in a mention of what they want and what they do, sprinkled with some hints of danger, and end with a question, a la "But can Empress Euphonia ever forgive gravedigger Gregor for what he did – and will she ever love again?"
7. Finally, give your novel a catchy title and design a jacket cover with, of course, the author's name prominently displayed on the spine. Print it out, wrap it around a book in your collection and leave it lying casually on the coffee table. Everyone will assume you've written the novel and voila, you'll get all of the glory with none (well, some) of the work.

A Cure For What Ails

8 of Pentacles

Many people mistakenly believe that Tarot cards – the Major Arcana in particular – have reached us in a state of total perfection. Yet nothing could be further from the truth. One accumulates a lot of baggage and bad habits in half a century. Fortunately, there's nothing a good laugh or a day at the spa can't cure…

1. Shuffle the Major Arcana cards, then hold them all in one hand, as though you're going to give them a good shake.
2. Give them a good shake.
3. Keep shaking until one or more cards fall to the ground (you might want to stand on a plush carpet to prevent bruising). These are the cards with the most baggage and which are most in need of your intervention.
4. Deal with one card at a time, starting with whichever looks the most desperate. Gaze at the card, with your head slightly tilted, first to the left then to the right. What do you make of the troubled soul in front of you? Breathe out through your nose, making a small sound as you do so. Imagine you are this card's closest friend and it's your job to decide what, exactly, is its problem?
5. Tell the card what its problem is. This will usually come out as, "You're too…………. You need to……………". As in, you're too rigid, you need to let it all hang out, man.
6. Once you've pinpointed where the card is going wrong, it's up to you to prescribe a course of treatment. What could you do – or what could the card do – to ease its suffering? For example, a card that is too blindly rational might benefit from a daily poetry reading, to soften some of those hard edges. A card that is too dark and drab might appreciate some beauty tips. A day at the zoo, a shopping spree, roller skating, The Three Stooges, a night at the opera – these are all ways in which you can help your cards shed hundreds of years' worth of psychological sediment.
7. After you've finished, you should notice that your cards seem lighter, more flexible and more radiant. Repeat the process every now and then to maintain their good mental health.

Dinner With Friends

9 of Pentacles

The Empress had created a feast to remember. The table was festooned with mouth-watering dishes cooked to perfection. As the High Priestess, the Magician, and Justice seated themselves, it seemed like nothing could go wrong. Then, suddenly, the Tower arrived...

1. Spread all the Major Arcana cards face down on a large dining table and swirl them around until they effervesce. Pick one at random.
2. You are going to hold a dinner party, this very evening at this very dining table, and the card you selected will help you make some important decisions. You must choose what theme you would like for your party, what to serve, and what dress code will be required – all based on the card you picked. If the card is willing, you might also consider some background music and decorations.
3. Once you have finished making all these crucial decisions, it's time to start preparations. Send out invitations. Cook or order in your menu. Blow up a large inflatable palm tree (but only if it suits your theme). PLACE YOUR MAJOR ARCANA CARDS IN THE CENTRE OF THE TABLE.
4. When your guests have arrived and are seated, clear your throat loudly to gain their attention. Announce that your Tarot cards will be responsible for keeping the conversation flowing tonight.
5. Starting with the guest who arrived first (because it's important to reward punctuality) ask each person in turn to shuffle the cards and pick one at random (or shuffle yourself and let your guests choose, if you're worried about others caressing your cards).
6. You must study the image and let it suggest an icebreaker. For example, if the Sun is chosen, you might ask everyone about their favorite childhood memory, or what they dreamed they'd be when they grew up. Or if Death is picked, you might ask if anyone's ever had a run-in with a machete-wielding skeleton.
7. Try to choose questions that will test your guests and provide the most scintillating small talk (see machete-wielding skeleton, above). Try to avoid questions that you already know the answers to (ditto).

8. Let every guest pick a card so that the conversation carries on throughout the meal. Afterwards, savor the feel-good feeling that comes from spending good times with good friends. And make sure all cards are returned before anyone leaves – just because they're your friends, doesn't mean they can be trusted.

Amateur Dramatics

10 of Pentacles

Like many theatrical plays, the Major Arcana is full of drama – and comedy and tragedy and confusing endings. Plus, there are extravagant costumes, elaborate sets, excruciatingly indulgent Death scenes. The majors should feel right at home on stage...

1. Pick one Major Arcana card.
2. Imagine you're responsible for set design on a big stage production. The card you hold in front of you is the director's vision. Your job is to recreate it on stage. You are not just building a set inspired by this card – you are building a set that looks *exactly like* this card.
3. It may help to think of the card in layers. Larger background elements would need to be placed at the back of the stage and the smaller foreground details would appear at the front of the stage. Think about textures, materials, and lighting. Imagine you have a limited budget to work with – what could you use or re-use to set the scene?
4. Now find a box, remove the lid or cut off the top flaps, and lay it on its side to make a stage. Your mission, should you choose to accept it, is to make a 3D version of the card, just as though you're building a theatrical set. Don't panic – no one is judging you (except Justice) and no one will laugh (except the Fool).
5. As much as possible, try to use things you already have around the house. Use food packaging to build structures (take the food out first, or better yet eat it). Cut up old magazines to get just the right color you need. Photograph objects that are too big or too valuable to be used and use cardboard cut-outs instead. Basically, cut, glue, and paint to your heart's content. You will find this easier if you have some preschoolers to help you.
6. When you've completed your set, give yourself a standing ovation. Think about what sort of story would take place on this stage. Keep your design and use it to help you write your masterpiece, "Tarot! – The Musical."

Angels and Demons

Page of Pentacles

It's a well-known fact* that there were originally 22 deadly sins, which were whittled down to seven after no one could be bothered to remember them all. And, of course, there were also 22 cardinal virtues, which were such a drag to live up to they were similarly culled. Nowadays, being able to name even seven virtues and sins is rare – unless you're training to be a quiz show contestant. The Tarot thinks it's time to raise the bar again…

1. Lay all 22 Major Arcana cards face up in front of you, in whatever arrangement you find most pleasing to the eye.
2. Pick a card at random and hold it with both hands. Focus on the image until everything else in the room goes all blurry and you start blinking a lot.
3. Now, access that deep part of yourself that your mother always swore was responsible for breaking her best china (your inner devil). Feel the magma bubble inside you and rise from your core, bringing with it a whole host of swear words you haven't heard since primary school. Project these feelings onto the card until it starts to scorch your fingertips.
4. Quickly, before the card bursts into flames, try to catch a whiff of its particular flavor of Deadly Sinfulness. What dark shadows lurk beneath its spiritual exterior? If it helps, turn the card upside down to make the sin fall out.
5. Make a note of what the card's deadly sin is – preferably distilling it down to just one word. So, for example, if you think the Hierophant looks like a smug old git, you could write "Self–Righteousness." Remember, this is not about what you think the card means.
6. Now blow on the card to put out the fire and to allow your inner Lucifer to cool off. Once calmed, open the top of your head to the heavens and allow the warm, bright rays of goodness to fill you up, traveling through your veins to the tips of your fingers and toes and the ends of your hair.
7. Again, project these feelings onto the card and wait for it to reflect them back to you. What cardinal virtue does the card extol? Imagine the card is preaching by example. Try to find the most

accurate and expressive word to describe it and then write it down – don't plump for any old keyword and don't just pick whatever is the opposite of the deadly sin. For example, maybe this time you write down "Devotion" for the Hierophant.

8. Do this for all 22 cards then submit your completed list of deadly sins and cardinal virtues to church leaders around the world, who will then rain blessings down upon you and your cards in thanks for your service to the greater good.

*Actually, it's complete fiction. As is the bit about the virtues.

The Fool's Journey: Redux

Knight of Pentacles

The Fool's Journey is a simple but powerful tale: An idiot falls off a cliff, meets lots of interesting people, and discovers the answer to life, the universe, and everything. Alas, reality isn't quite as straightforward, which is why Tarot was made into cards, not a book…

1. Find the Fool and place him, her, or it in front of you.
2. Shuffle the rest of the Major Arcana and arrange them face down below the Fool in three rows of seven.
3. Starting at the top left, turn the cards face up to reveal each step of the Fool's New Journey. Imagine the Fool meeting each of these cards in turn (or encountering what they represent). Imagine the setting in which each meeting happens and what propels the Fool from one scene to the next. It might help to think of each encounter as a mini-quest, with each Major Arcana card sending the Fool off to complete a task which will lead him to the next card. Or you could imagine that the first card in each row sets a quest and the remaining cards in each row help the Fool to complete it.
4. The last card represents the Fool's ultimate destiny so give it special consideration. What has he learned since his journey began? What has he gained and what has he lost? How is he different to the Fool who set out at the beginning?

Part Five

Forever Friends

2 Small Ways to Show You Care

The Final Curtain

Queen of Pentacles

And now, the end is near – the end of this book that is. You and your deck are just beginning. You're young and – hopefully – in love, and you have your whole lives ahead of you. But what if – I can hardly write the words – what if the worse should happen? What if your cards were snatched by a giant eagle, or eroded by sulfuric acid, or accidentally flushed down the toilet? Sometimes you don't appreciate a good thing until it's gone...

1. Cover a small box (such as a shoebox) in a black cloth and place your deck on it with the Death card facing up.
2. Light a few candles and play some somber background music.
3. Stand before your deck and – with bottom lip trembling and upper lip stiff – recall the things you loved about your deck. What special memories do you have of your time together? What did you always secretly admire about it? What will you miss the most? Sing its praises without reserve – you may never get another chance.
4. When you've said all you can, blow out each candle one by one and stop the music. Bow your head and observe a minute's silence.
5. Fortunately, you're just pretending; so now it's over, pick up your cards and give them a big hug. Celebrate being alive. Throw open the windows, throw confetti, throw a party (but don't throw your cards). Shuffle the Death card back into the pack in favor of Judgement and give thanks for the second shot at happiness.

Present Time

King of Pentacles

Well, here you are, 78 times closer to your deck than you were when you started. Think of all the happy times you've shared – playing, dancing, drawing, prancing, roller skating, and raising the dead. Never has a human being bonded so tightly with a few small pieces of cardboard (well, not without the aid of some glue). You and your cards are strong enough to take on the world – but before you do, there's one last thing to take care of…

1. This is very simple: All you have to do is buy your deck a gift. You can buy it a silk bag, a velvet pillow, a pair of sparkly earrings, a work of art – whatever you feel is appropriate. The only rule is that it be something special that you buy specifically for this deck (so no digging out some old watch that used to belong to your uncle).
2. Take the time to wrap your gift carefully and to make it look beautiful. Imagine it's a gift for a loved one (which it is). Tie a ribbon around it. Write a little note to go with it.
3. Pick a special time and place to give your deck its gift. Make sure you are alone. Tell it that you value its friendship and that you want to give it something to show how much you care. Read the note if you wrote one, then unwrap the gift and give it to your deck.
4. The gift you've given now belongs to your deck. This part is very important. It's not yours – you do not own it any more than you own your cards. It must stay with or near your deck. You are not allowed to sell it, trade it, or discard it unless you sell, trade, or discard your cards. (Oh, the horror!).
5. Accept nothing from your deck in return but the warm glow of mutual affection and next week's lottery numbers if it knows them.

Playlists

Things to Do With Non-Scenic Pips
(52 activities)

Decks with non-scenic pips are used to getting a raw deal. Shunned by the masses, misunderstood by outsiders and beginners alike, NSPs rarely get more than a cursory mention in Tarot books. But all are welcome here. If your deck is pictorially-challenged, there are still a whopping 52 novel ways you can connect with them.

Look at the following description and corresponding page numbers!

Page	Activity		Page	Activity
12	Committed		66	Two Become One
30	Drawing Closer		72	Wishful Thinking
40	Cryptarotography		82	In the Mood
46	Whodunit		84	E.S.P.
50	Through the Peephole		87	All of Part Three
52	The Sound of Silence		119	All of Part Four
54	A Rose By Any Other		166	The Final Curtain
62	Rain or Shine		168	Present Time

Things to Do in a Hurry
(18 activities)

Overslept? Late for work? Don't take it out on your deck. Set a timer for five minutes and pick just one of the activities on this list. Sure, you might get fired, but your deck will appreciate your dedication.

Page	Activity
22	Voices in Your Head
26	Taroga
28	Split Personality

Page	Activity
33	Cliffhangers
42	Scratch and Sniff
44	Little White Book
60	Literal Thinking
68	Remember Remember
74	Excuse Me ("Reasons why you are late for work," "Reasons why your boss shouldn't fire you")
90	The Great Pretender
106	Strike Up the Band
114	King for a Day
122	Between the Lines
126	A You're Adorable
130	Dancing With the Devil
142	Instant Expert
154	A Cure for What Ails
160	Angels & Demons

Things to Do With Friends
(9 activities)

Tarot can be a solitary business. Much time is spent alone, in silence, with only your cards for company. Whilst it would be difficult to truly bond with your deck if you're forever in a crowd, the occasional addition of a select few Tarot-reading friends will spice up your relationship and keep things interesting. See the following pages for multi-player rules.

Page	Activity
108	Off With Their Heads
120	A Town Called Tarot
130	Dancing With the Devil
132	Rude Rhymes
144	Face Off
146	The Old School Tie
156	Dinner With Friends
158	Amateur Dramatics
166	The Final Curtain

Off With Their Heads!

Make one copy of the cards for each person. Cut up and mix as per instructions (keep each person's copies separate). Compete to see who can reassemble their courts the quickest and who can create the best "stitched–together" courts.

A Town Called Tarot

You'll need a much larger piece of paper. Give everyone some crayons; then enact scenarios with each person puppeteering one or more cards (townsfolk).

Rude Rhymes

Choose one card. Who can come up with the funniest/quickest/rudest/best limerick?

Dancing With the Devil

Throw on a mix-tape and make it a party! Dance as if no one is watching, even though they are.

Face Off

Divide the Major Arcana between you and a friend. Choose one attribute before each reveals a card. The winner gets to keep both cards. Keep playing until one player holds all the cards or the whole thing has degenerated into a wrestling match.

The Old School Tie

Each person chooses a different card. Compete to see who can design the best emblem. Or work together to see how many different emblems you can create from the same card.

Dinner With Friends

This should be self-explanatory.

Amateur Dramatics

With friends you can work on a much grander scale. Build a life-size replica of the Tower in your living room, using only materials you have on hand.

The Final Curtain

Invite your friends and their decks to pay their respects. Ask each one to say a few words or perhaps read a favorite passage or poem.

Sensible Things to Do With Serious Decks (22 activities)

Some decks just don't do silly. If this is your deck, it's important that you respect its wishes and don't force it to do anything that would make it uncomfortable. Use this list of incredibly sensible and grown-up activities instead.

Page	Activity
14	Twenty Questions
16	First Impressions
28	Split Personality
30	Drawing Closer
36	The Whole Enchilada
40	Cryptarotography
50	Through the Peephole
52	The Sound of Silence
64	Making Headlines

Card Index

Let your deck bring the fun in! Shuffle your cards, draw one at random, then use the index below to discover what you and your cards will be doing next.

Card	Activity	Page
2 of Swords	The Dark Side	112
3 of Swords	King for a Day	114
4 of Swords	Behind Closed Doors	116
5 of Swords	A Town Called Tarot	120
6 of Swords	Between the Lines	122
7 of Swords	The House That Tarot Built	124
8 of Swords	*A* You're Adorable	126
9 of Swords	Everything Counts	128
10 of Swords	Dancing With the Devil	130
Page of Swords	Rude Rhymes	132
Knight of Swords	Skin Deep	134
Queen of Swords	Outside the Box	136
King of Swords	Wisdom of the Majors	138
Ace of Pentacles	The Devil's in the Details	140
2 of Pentacles	Instant Expert	142
3 of Pentacles	Face Off	144
4 of Pentacles	The Old School Tie	146
5 of Pentacles	Religious Zeal	148
6 of Pentacles	Personal Effects	150
7 of Pentacles	A Novel Approach	152
8 of Pentacles	A Cure For What Ails	154
9 of Pentacles	Dinner With Friends	156
10 of Pentacles	Amateur Dramatics	158
Page of Pentacles	Angels and Demons	160
Knight of Pentacles	The Fool's Journey: Redux	162
Queen of Pentacles	The Final Curtain	166
King of Pentacles	Present Time	168